Spirit of the Wild Dog

Lesley J. Rogers and **Gisela Kaplan** are professors at the University of New England, Armidale, New South Wales. They have conducted joint research in the field of animal behaviour for many years and have published together both books and scientific papers. Their co-authored books include *Birds: Their Habits and Skills* (2001), *The Orang-utans* (1999) and *Not Only Roars and Rituals: Communication in Animals* (1998). Both have been influenced by their field research, observing birds, apes and dogs in their natural habitats.

Lesley J. Rogers has a Doctor of Philosophy and a Doctor of Science from the University of Sussex and is an elected Fellow of the Australian Academy of Science. Her area of research is neuroscience and animal behaviour, and has covered a wide range of species from lower vertebrates to apes. She has a leading international reputation for her research on brain development and behaviour. In addition to the above books, she has published *Minds of Their Own: Thinking and Awareness in Animals* (1997) and recently, with R.J. Andrew, *Comparative Vertebrate Lateralization* (2002).

Gisela Kaplan has a Doctor of Philosophy from Monash University. She was foundation professor of social sciences at Queensland University and is now research professor at the University of New England, in both biological sciences and education. A prolific writer, she has authored over a hundred research articles and fourteen books. She also contributes to wildlife magazines, community education and media science programs. She has rehabilitated native Australian wildlife for nearly a decade. Her fields of research include animal communication, cognition and animal welfare.

Spirit of the Wild Dog

The world of wolves, coyotes,
foxes, jackals & dingoes

Lesley J. Rogers & Gisela Kaplan

ALLEN&UNWIN

Photo credits: pp. vi, 164 Gisela Kaplan; p. xii Nigel Dennis, ANT Photo
Library; p. 16 Getty Images; p. 40 Terry Whittaker, Frank Lane Picture
Agency/Corbis; p. 58 James Gritz, Getty Images; p.86 Getty Images;
p. 106 Gerard Lacz, ANT Photo Library; p. 120 Peter Johnson, Corbis;
p. 144 Alan and Sandy Carey, Getty Images; p. 182 Tom Brakefield, Corbis.

First published in 2003

Allen & Unwin
83 Alexander Street
Crows Nest NSW 2065
Australia
Phone: (61 2) 8425 0100
Fax: (61 2) 9906 2218
Email: info@allenandunwin.com
Web: www.allenandunwin.com

National Library of Australia
Cataloguing-in-Publication entry:

Rogers, Lesley J. (Lesley Joy), 1943- .
   Spirit of the wild dog: The world of wolves, coyotes, foxes, jackals
   & dingoes.

   Bibliography.
   Includes index.
   ISBN 1 86508 673 8.

   1. Wild dogs. I. Kaplan, Gisela. II. Title.

599.772

Set in 10.85/15 pt Stempel Garamond by Bookhouse, Sydney
Printed by Griffin Press, South Australia

10 9 8 7 6 5 4 3 2

Contents

Acknowledgements

We are grateful to Robert Harden, Research Officer for the National Parks and Wildlife Service, for many discussions on dingoes and for providing us with some of the literature; to Rebecca Conn for help in preparing the index; to Nicola Cross for her assistance in collecting the reference material; and to Craig Lawlor for preparing the distribution maps. We wish to pay tribute to the many staff all around the world who work tirelessly in the field to save remnant populations of wild dogs from extinction. We have been fortunate to visit Botswana and Krüger National Park in Africa and Bandipur and Nagarole National Parks in India. In particular, we thank our guides in Bandipur for helping us see wild dogs in their natural environment. The latter experience, perhaps more than any other, inspired us to write this book. We also thank our publisher, Ian Bowring, and editor, Colette Vella, as well as the rest of the team at Allen & Unwin, for their encouragement and advice.

We dedicate this book to the memory of Jenny, the alpha female in our own Rhodesian ridgeback pack, and her surviving siblings, Luke and Julie. They have allowed us to join their clan and were with us throughout the writing of this book.

Preface

Sometimes small events can have lasting impact. For Lesley Rogers, this was seeing a wild dog for the first time. It was many years ago, at dusk and in South Australia. The first sighting had been fleeting and might have been forgotten as a case of mistaken identity if it had not been seen a second time. The dog appeared suddenly on a sloping hillside, looked around and then, with a number of leaps, disappeared into its den. Seeing it enter its den showed beyond all doubt that this special animal was wild, living independently of humans. In the diminishing light Lesley had seen a free spirit and, for a moment, experienced an aspect of dogs she had not even imagined before, despite a life-long and deep association with pet dogs.

When Gisela Kaplan was nine years old her grandmother took her to the zoo in Berlin. On a footpath, very nearly underfoot, there was a little fox pup. It was tied to a fence post with an incongruously large chain, and it was all on its own. The fox pup was lying on its side, eyes closed. Gisela's grandmother said: 'Come on, you can pat the fox. It will probably like it, but be gentle.' Overjoyed, Gisela crouched down and patted the fox. The fur was so soft, so fluffy, and underneath it she could feel the fox breathing. She was mesmerised when the fox first opened its large beautiful eyes, then lifted its head, turned it and slowly and deliberately licked her hand. She decided that this was the most beautiful and loving animal she had ever met (not that she had met many at this young age) but a very deep, heart-wrenching sorrow came over her almost instantly. The sorrow was a mix of knowing that she had to leave it behind and knowing that there was nothing she could do to free it of the chains weighing heavily on its tiny neck. She wanted to take it with her. She wanted it to be free and respected instead of ignored.

It was not entirely by chance that we acquired four large Rhodesian ridgeback dogs. When our Rhodesian ridgeback mother was a four-week-old pup, she was of a low rank amidst a litter of thirteen. We visited the owners who wanted to sell the pups. Gisela put her hand into the box containing the whelping litter and a little pup moved towards her. She picked her up and held her for a moment. The pup had a little white tip on her tail and was therefore easily distinguished from the others. We went away, but this experience stayed so much with us that we decided to check on the pups a week later. The same thing happened: the little white-tipped pup once again scrambled towards Gisela, this time whining softly and snuggling up to her hand. An instant bond was formed. Unlike that little fox of Gisela's childhood, this dog could be taken home.

We named the pup Tipsy. She grew into an exceptionally loving dog and there came a time when we thought it unbearable to lose her. So she was mated and produced four live pups. The care of the pups was left to Tipsy but when she suffered septicaemia, a bottle had to take the place of nipples. Suckling four pups was a time-consuming task but it afforded an intimacy that built more than just trust. We had intended to keep just one pup but, after the extensive feeding schedule over many weeks, selling or giving them away was no longer an option. They had become part of the family and, except for one pup who went to close friends, they grew up with their mother. They became a firm family unit, inseparable and exceptionally fair to each other. We learned to respect their social rules and mimicked them in our behaviour to them. We became part of their pack by their own generous admission and we cannot think of a happier time than has been spent with these proud and faithful dogs.

ONE

An African wild dog,
Lycaon pictus.

The wild dog family

Our own trusted pet dogs are in some ways a far cry from their relatives in the wild. Over some 100 000 years of living with humans, the dogs we know so well have adapted their behaviour to complement our lifestyles. When tamed and under our control, we love them, but as free spirits, in the wild, dogs seem to feature more readily as our enemy.

Humans have long been on the warpath against wild dogs. We have hunted, shot, trapped and poisoned them out of fear, for recreation, to protect our flocks and to make fur coats. Yet, we live with and nurture their relatives, domestic dogs.

It is, perhaps, easy to see why farmers resort to killing wild dogs after they have seen their sheep viciously attacked and torn apart; or why people take revenge if a wild dog attacks a human, whatever the provocation or circumstances. All too often this results in retaliatory killing that far exceeds the 'crime'. Killing sprees and mass poisonings have all but eliminated many wild dog populations. Yet, those remaining wild dogs survive with a spirit we can only respect. How much of it do we understand?

Characteristics of dogs

Dogs are a diverse group of species belonging to the family Canidae. Some people use the label 'wild dog' to refer only to domestic dogs that have become wild living animals, but the wild dogs of the Canidae family include wolves, coyotes, foxes, jackals, dingoes and many other species.

The Canidae are ground-living carnivores with mouths and teeth adapted for killing prey or tearing apart flesh. In particular, they have strong jaw muscles and their jaws are large enough in most species to accommodate forty-two teeth. Four of the teeth, the canine teeth, are enlarged and pointed so that they can hold prey efficiently. The dog's mouth is used primarily for manipulating things. In fact, their mouth is a multipurpose structure used for eating, 'handling' things and for communicating both vocally and by touch (licking and biting). Although meat is their main food, most dogs eat some forms of vegetation as well—foxes, for example, eat fruit and are particularly partial to blackberries. Also, wolves often eat small rodents and the bat-eared fox of Africa feeds mainly on insects.

The canids (as we call the Canidae) are excellent runners. Many are light and swift with long and slender limbs, compared to the size of their body. These characteristics serve them well in hunting and when escaping from animals that prey on them. There are exceptions to this body design, such as the stubby little bush dog of South America, which stands only 30 centimetres tall at the shoulder. These dogs are perfectly adapted for swimming. Similar to little corgis, they can move swiftly in water, where they hunt large water rodents, the paca and capybara.

Wild dogs are characterised by their well-developed tails, which are longer in those species that hunt large prey. The tail assists the dog to make sharp turns at high speeds, and is important for communicating to other members of the pack during hunting and other social interactions.

The dog's paws are also adapted for running down prey. They run on their toes using all four limbs. This differs from their nearest relatives the bears who use their heels, and sit or walk on their hind limbs alone. Although pet dogs are often taught to sit or walk like this, it is not a behaviour that dogs perform naturally. Dogs use their front paws to hold down their food or other objects, and also to grip fellow dogs in play and other social interactions. The presence of dew claws on the front limbs also helps in holding down prey or objects.

The dog's claws do not retract, like cat-claws. This characteristic reflects the fact that dogs, with the exception of the grey fox (or tree-climbing fox), do not use their paws for climbing trees or killing prey. Whereas a cat can kill large prey on its own, dogs need to do so by hunting in packs. The less sociable members of the family that hunt alone take smaller prey.

The different species of dogs

There are thirty-six species of Canidae, although some debates on their classification vary this number slightly. These species are fitted into fifteen categories, each of which is known as a genus (see Appendix). In other words, each genus is divided into a number of different species.

The largest and probably the best-known genus is *Canis*, which includes three of the four wolves in the Canidae family (the grey wolf *Canis lupus*; red wolf, *Canis rufus* and Ethiopian wolf, *Canis simensis*), all of the three jackals (the golden jackal, *Canis aureus*; black-backed jackal, *Canis mesomelas* and side-striped jackal, *Canis adustus*), the coyote (*Canis latrans*), the dingo (*Canis familiaris* (or *lupus*) *dingo*), the New Guinea singing dog (*Canis familiaris* (or *lupus*) *hallstromi*) and the domestic dog (*Canis familiaris domesticus*). The dingo of Australia and the New Guinea singing dog can be classified in two ways: some people say that the dingo and the singing dog are variants of the domestic dog, and so use 'familiaris' in the name; others see them as being more closely related to the wolf and refer instead to *'lupus'*. All of the members of this genus are highly social animals and, in the wild, all suffer the demise of declining numbers.

The second largest genus is *Vulpes*, which includes the foxes of Europe, Africa, Asia and the Middle East and the kit fox (*Vulpes velox*) of North America. The most familiar member of this genus is the red fox, *Vulpes vulpes*, from which the fox fur stoles and capes worn by our mothers and grandmothers were made. This species inhabits Europe, Asia, North America, small areas of northern Africa and, since its introduction over one hundred years ago, Australia.

The seven other members of the genus *Vulpes* include the pale fox (*Vulpes pallida*), Cape fox (*Vulpes chama*), Bengal fox (*Vulpes bengalensis*), Rüppell's fox (*Vulpes rueppelli*), Steppe fox (*Vulpes corsac*), Tibetan fox (*Vulpes ferrilata*) and Blanford's fox (*Vulpes cana*).

The grey fox and island fox of the American continent are in another genus, *Urocyon*. Grey foxes are spread from Canada to the northern tip of South America, whereas the island fox is limited to parts of California. Due to their distinguishing features, notably their large ears, fennec foxes have their own genus and species, *Fennecus zerda*; the same applies to the bat-eared fox, whose genus and species is *Otocyon megalotis*.

The Arctic fox, *Alopex lagopus*, is unique largely in terms of the environment it inhabits, and it is the only member of this genus.

The third main genus of Canidae is *Dusicyon*, to which six of the seven foxes of South America belong. (This genus is sometimes divided into three: *Pseudalopex, Atelocynus* and *Lycalopex*, which is why we say there are fifteen categories of genus in the family Canidae.) These foxes are known also as zorros, the common South American name for fox, and the six species in this genus are: the Santa Helena zorro (also known as the culpeo), *Dusicyon culpaeus*; grey zorro, *Dusciyon griseus*; pampas fox, *Dusciyon gymnocerus*; Sechuran fox or zorro, *Dusciyon sechurae*; small-eared zorro, *Dusciyon microtis*; and hoary zorro, *Dusciyon vetulus*.

The only other fox found in South America, the crab-eating zorro, named after the crustacean it enjoys devouring, has its own genus and species, *Cerdocyon thous*. South America is also home to the bush dog, whose swimming prowess, mentioned above, warrants its own genus and species, *Speothos venaticus*.

Some very important members of the family Canidae are the African wild dog, *Lycaon pictus*, and the Asiatic wild dog or dhole, *Cuon alpinus*, both of which, as their scientific names show, belong to a separate genus. Genetic studies have shown that they are both related to the wolves.

The remaining two categories of the Canidae, which each have only one species, are *Chrysocyon brachyurus*, the maned wolf, and *Nyctereutes procyonoides*, the raccoon dog.

The classification of Canidae becomes more complex when we consider the subspecies. Nearly all of the species are divided further into a number of subspecies. The red fox, *Vulpes vulpes*, has the largest number with a total of forty-four subspecies, and the grey wolf, *Canis lupus*, has at least twenty-six subspecies. Already seven subspecies of the grey wolf have become extinct, as has the white wolf of Newfoundland and the Shamanu of Japan, both subspecies of *Canis lupus*.

The evolution of dogs

The family Canidae separated from the rest of the carnivores to form its own line of evolution about 40 to 50 million years ago in the geological period known as the Eocene, and the canids appeared first in the continent of North America. This means that they appeared long after the mass extinction of the dinosaurs, which took place 65 million years ago. The first members of Canidae were more like present-day raccoons, mongooses, genets or civets than the wild dogs we know today. They were carnivores like present-day dogs, but their limbs were still adapted for climbing trees. Therefore, they could not run rapidly on open ground.

The canid line of evolution continued in North America and gave rise to many different branches—all closely related—about 10 to 15 million years ago. These canids spread across a land bridge, spanning what we now call the Bering Strait, from North America into

Eurasia about 5 to 7 million years ago, then fanned out across the Eurasian continent. On their arrival in Eurasia the canids encountered relatives called the 'half dogs', or amphi-cyonids, which died out soon afterwards, probably because they had to compete against the more successful true dogs, the Canidae, in climatic conditions that had changed considerably. The temperature had fallen and grasslands had spread into areas that had been wooded before. The Canidae were ideally suited to living in these new conditions and they were quick to adapt their diets to take advantage of available foods. At the same time, antelopes evolved and dogs exploited them as a food source by hunting in packs.

It was about this time that all of the existing modern canids began to diverge from a common ancestor and became, eventually, the wolves, coyotes, jackals, foxes and other wild dogs that we know today. Some of the canids that evolved in Eurasia moved back across the Bering land bridge into North America. A hare-eating coyote did so about 2 million years ago and it later gave rise to the present-day coyotes. The grey wolf, it is thought, evolved in Eurasia about 3 million years ago but it did not move across into North America until about 700 000 years ago.

One and a half million years ago, three separate lineages of wolves roamed the earth. These were the grey wolves (*Canis lupus*), the dire wolves (*Canis dirus*) and the red wolves (*Canis rufus*), although there are differing opinions on the time when red wolves evolved.

The wild dog family

The dire wolves, it seems, still ranged from Canada to Peru about 18 000 years ago, at a time when humans first reached the New World via the Bering Strait or land bridge. They became extinct about 10 000 years ago. Thousands of skeletons of the dire wolf have been found in tar pits near Los Angeles. Many animals were trapped in these pools of tar resulting from oil that had surfaced from underground. Once they had walked or fallen into them the animals were doomed and long after death their bones remained preserved as a record of evolution.

The dire wolf looked much like the grey wolf, with whom it coexisted. It weighed about 50 kilograms and was 1.5 metres from head to tip of tail, but its head was larger and heavier, its teeth were larger, probably used to crush bone, and its legs were sturdier. The dire wolf must have been an impressive predator but some say that it was primarily a scavenger, like the hyena is today. Its extinction was probably caused by a change in the climate, which led to the disappearance of its prey. It is known that many other mammals became extinct at this same time. Apparently, the dire wolf was unable to adapt to eating different prey, whereas the other wolves were able to do so.

The evolution of the foxes belonging to the genus *Vulpes* followed a separate branch. The red fox is typical of these and it evolved in Eurasia and spread from there to North America and to Africa, adapting to form new species, and also foxes of different genera, as each new environment was encountered. To mention but two, the

Fennec fox of the Sahara, with its enormous ears, and the Cape fox from the southern tip of Africa evolved in this way from a red fox ancestor.

About half a million years ago the canids became social and started to hunt in groups. One such dog, *Canis falconeri*, evolved in the western fringe of Europe and discovery of its remains in Spain has revealed that these dogs weighed about 30 kilograms. Judging by their teeth and the dimensions of their jaw and skull, it appears that their diet was less oriented to meat than the diet of most canids today but, nevertheless, the species seems to have hunted in cooperation with group members. Another species, *Canis etruscus*, living in the same place at the same time consumed more meat in its diet but it weighed only about 10 kilograms.

An important point in the classification of dogs is the fact that the various species of *Canis* can, and do, interbreed. One influential definition of a species is on the basis that the members of one species cannot interbreed with the members of another species to give fertile offspring. This definition has not been applied to the classification of canids. Their ability to interbreed has important consequences for efforts to protect populations of dogs in the wild and explains why there is much debate about the definition of some dog species. In such cases, classification into separate species is generally based on physical characteristics that distinguish one group from another. Of these, the teeth and structure of the skull are particularly important. Modern techniques that can determine the differences and similarities of the genetic material are also useful in classifying species. Such studies can shed some light on whether a type is really a distinct species or a hybrid between two species.

Interbreeding and the difficulties it causes for classification is highlighted by the debate about the the red wolf, *Canis rufus*, of North America, and whether it is a separate species in its own right or merely a hybrid resulting from crossbreeding of the grey wolf and the coyote. A study by Robert Wayne and his colleagues found that the sequences of genes in the red wolf were not distinctly different from those of the coyote on one hand and the grey wolf on the other and so concluded that red wolves are not a separate species but a hybrid between coyotes and grey wolves. The conclusion reached from this study was that, possibly as recently as European settlement of North America, the grey wolves in south-central United States bred with coyotes and so formed the red wolves. This might have come about because the presence of the settlers caused the numbers of grey wolves to decline and then some of the grey wolves began to breed with coyotes.

However, not all scientists accept this theory and those who disagree suggest that the red wolf had its own independent line of evolution that, some say, may have separated from the coyote some 150 000 to 300 000 years ago. A recent genetic study of red wolves and the grey wolf of eastern Canada, carried out by Paul Wilson and colleagues, found genetic similarities between the eastern

Canadian wolf and the red wolf, despite the fact that theses two types of wolf occur on opposite sides of the North American continent. They also found similarities between the genetic material of both these species and the coyote but not the grey wolf. Therefore, these researchers suggested that both the eastern Canadian wolf and the red wolf evolved from an ancestral coyote and that the red wolf is a separate species in its own right. Further research is needed to clarify these differences.

Domestication of dogs

Latest evidence suggests that the grey wolf, *Canis lupus*, started to associate with humans and become domesticated some 135 000 years ago. This was about, or just after, the time when modern humans, that is, *Homo sapiens*, evolved.

The beginning of domestication of the dog was earlier than any other domestic species. The chicken, for example, was domesticated only about 5000 to 8000 years ago, the cat about 7000 years ago and the horse as recently as 5000 to 6000 years ago.

All of our modern domestic dog-breeds appear to have come from one ancestral species (*Canis lupus*), as shown by comparison of the hereditary material (mitochondrial DNA) from different dog species, wild and domestic, throughout the world. The DNA of domestic dogs was found to be closer to that of the wolves than to either coyotes or jackals. Such comparisons, which were carried out by Carles Vila, Robert Wayne and a number of colleagues in 1997, also indicate that at least four independent events of domestication may have taken place, but the number could be higher. The four events of domestication were suggested since the domestic dogs examined could be categorised into four groups on the basis of similar DNA. The study found that the largest group contained many of the domestic breeds, including basenjis, collies, border collies, greyhounds and boxers. This group also included the dingo and the singing dog of New Guinea. Group two contained the Scandinavian elkhound and another Scandinavian breed, called the jämthund, and the DNA of this group was related closely the wolves of Italy, Greece, France and Romania. The third group contained German shepherds, Siberian huskies and the Mexican hairless dog (or Xoloitzcuintli). The fourth group was very closely related to the wolves of Romania and western Russia and contained, amongst others, the Tibetan spaniel, Afghan hound and golden retriever.

Although these results may be said to show that dogs were domesticated several times, each in a different part of the world, it could also mean that domestication took place only once and later different groups of domestic dogs bred with wolves. This possibility may explain why modern domestic dogs are more genetically varied than other domestic animals, especially cats. Most likely both processes occurred—that is, more than one event of domestication took place and later some domesticated dogs interbred with wolves. Nevertheless, the fact that the majority of domestic breeds tested by Vila and colleagues fell into one group (group one) suggests that the domestication of dogs occurred as rather rare events and that there might have been one such main event.

As most wild dogs can interbreed with domestic dogs, it is possible that even coyotes and jackals interbred with some of the domestic dogs but, so far, the evidence shows that wolves were the main ancestors of domestic dogs. Only when the DNA of all breeds of domestic dogs is examined will we know with certainty whether they have interbred with other species of wild dog. In addition, this DNA study, which has been the main one so far, looked only at the DNA passed on by mothers (that is, mito-chondrial DNA) and this would not detect whether interbreeding had occurred between female domestic dogs and male coyotes or jackals. However, a prelimi-nary study examining the latter (using DNA from the cell nucleus) supports the conclusion that the wolf is the ancestor of the domestic dogs.

Ray Coppinger, an expert on dogs and their evolu-tion, suggests that domestication of the dog began when wolves chose to stay around the camps of nomadic humans, where they were able to feed on discarded food scraps and waste material. In other words, the dogs chose to be with, or at least near, us rather than the other way round. In time, the bond between humans and dogs grew and these dogs began to change in appearance, but this did not happen until about 12 000 to 14 000 years ago.

Prior to that time the dogs associating with humans did not differ in appearance from wolves, although their behaviour might have been different. We have no way of telling what their behaviour was from either their fossil records or by using modern genetic techniques. It is probable though that the original wolves that chose to stay near humans were not as shy or aggressive as wolves in general.

Dogs slowly and surely became part of human society and probably changed in appearance because humans started to intervene in their breeding—that is, to select dogs with certain physical and behavioural characteristics. This led to distinct changes in the appearance of domestic dogs, as can be seen in the skeletons of dogs from archaeological sites (see Chapter 9).

TWO

An Arctic fox, *Alopex lagopus*,
hunting for prey under the snow.

Habitats of
the wild dog

Wild dogs inhabit every continent of the world except the Antarctic: they have adapted to living in the driest and hottest parts of Africa and Australia, the wettest forests of South America and New Guinea and the coldest parts of the Arctic Circle. Some species alone cover a surprisingly large range of habitats. This is especially true of the red fox and the Asiatic wild dog, also known as the dhole. A large part of the range of the red fox covers the continents of Europe and Asia, from the coldest north to the hottest south, in some places that are very arid regions and other that are always wet. The range of the Asiatic wild dog extends from the cold Steppes of Siberia through regions of the Himalayas and southwards to the tropics of India and even the steaming rainforests of Java.

Habitat has an important influence on the behaviour of wild dogs and, in general, the larger wild dogs inhabit regions where their prey is readily available, whereas the smaller wild dogs live in regions where their prey is less abundant, at least at certain times of the year. For example, the fennec fox inhabits the desert areas of North Africa, where food is insufficient year round to support a large body size; whereas larger canids, such as the grey wolf and the African wild dog, inhabit regions where food is always more readily available (at least, that was the case in the past). In other words, the size of wild dogs adapted to food availability over evolutionary time.

Compared with other species, many canid species have unusual abilities to adapt to different habitats when their survival and food supply is threatened. This goes hand in hand with their ability to adapt to eating a wide range of food and to hunting over a variety of terrains. With these qualities the wild dogs have been long-term survivors over millions of years—that is, until humans began to threaten their existence. Although only one species of wild dog, the Falkland Island wolf, has become extinct in the last 400 years, many other species of wild dogs are now hovering at the edge of extinction.

Being few in number makes the chances of survival of a species very low indeed. Only a few Mexican wolves, *Canis lupus baileyi*, still exist in the wild. They are a subspecies of the grey wolf and once inhabited parts of the south-west of the United States as well as Mexico. Captive breeding and reintroduction of these wolves into the wild is taking place. It remains to be seen how successful such measures will be in re-establishing the wild population but the aim is to maximise their genetic diversity as much as possible by breeding as many different individuals with each other as possible. That way, it is hoped, the species might manage to expand and survive in the wild.

Wolves and the coyote

The grey wolf once roamed in large numbers throughout Europe and Asia, as well as almost all of North America and the western side of Greenland (Figure 2.1). Without its freedom curtailed, it adapted to living in a broad range of habitats, although these did not include tropical rain forests or arid deserts. There are only about 300 000 grey wolves alive today—genetic studies suggest that the population size of the grey wolf has declined recently in evolutionary time. The species now has a much smaller area of distribution which is confined to remote areas far away from human habitation and activities. Added to this, the density of the grey wolves is very low throughout their current distribution. Even though grey wolves can be found over much of their former range in India, for example, they are now so rare that possibly no more than a few hundred survive there.

Grey wolves are no longer found in the British Isles, the last ones being exterminated in the 1700s, and they have also disappeared from 75 per cent of continental

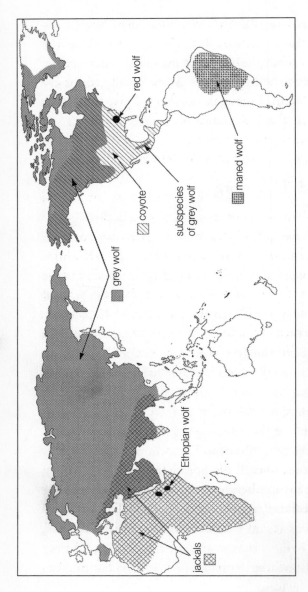

Figure 2.1: Distribution of wolves, the coyote and jackals.

The shaded areas indicate the approximate current distributions of the jackals and those species that are at least sometimes, if not always, referred to as wolves. The coyote is sometimes called the prairie wolf or brush wolf. The Ethiopian wolf (two black spots in north-east Africa) is also known as the Ethiopian jackal or the Simien jackal. Apart from the latter species, there are three species of jackals: black-backed, side-striped and golden jackals. The distribution of these three species is indicated collectively. The black-backed, also known as the silver-backed, jackal occurs at the southern tip of Africa southward from the Gulf of Aden. The side-striped jackal occurs in central Africa. The golden, also known as Asiatic, jackal is distributed through North Africa and across the Middle East through India and on to Indochina. Note that these distributions tell us nothing of the numbers of animals in any region. The grey wolf, for example, now occurs only sparsely throughout its range.

European countries. By the early 1900s, grey wolves had been eliminated from most of Western Europe and also Japan. In Europe the only remaining significant numbers of wolves are in the Balkans but a few small groups can be found in Spain, Portugal, northern Italy, the Czech Republic, Poland and Scandinavia.

The decline of their numbers in North America was more recent and more rapid. In some areas of their range, wolves have not been seen for some time and, for example, in parts of Canada the density is as low as one wolf per 500 square kilometres. In other areas, such as around the Great Lakes, the density is about one wolf per 30 square kilometres and many other areas have sufficient resources to maintain much higher densities than they currently do. The main regions of North America in which wolves occur today are Alaska, Canada, Minnesota, Wisconsin and a few adjoining regions. The population in Greenland died out in the 1930s but some have made their way back from the far northern regions of Canada.

In contrast to the above figures, numbers of the grey wolf have increased in the former USSR, as agriculture practices have changed, and in north-west Spain. Despite these exceptions, overall the populations of grey wolves are declining in numbers even in countries where they have been declared a protected species. The problem seems to be not just the loss of suitable prey (deer and, in North America, caribou and moose) and habitat but also the negative regard in which humans hold them. As a result of the latter, grey wolves are still killed in substantial numbers. In Alaska, for example, the grey wolf is still hunted legally as a sport and the hunters use snow mobiles and aircraft to reach the wolves. Here hunting has been the most significant reason for the declining numbers. Aerial means of hunting wolves is also exercised in areas of Russia and so is poisoning. This is justified on the basis that it keeps the numbers under control and so allows ungulates (moose and caribou in Alaska) to expand their numbers, but it is a controversial practice. Thousands of grey wolves are killed every year in this way and populations remain low as a result. A study conducted on wolves in Yukon, Canada, found that within six years of the cessation of aerial killing their numbers increased from around thirty to over 200. This shows that there could be a reversal of their present demise.

Packs of grey wolves range over areas that vary in size depending on the season of the year and availability of food. There have been reports of range sizes of tens, hundreds and even thousands of square kilometres. These ranges are determined by putting a radio transmitter collar on at least one wolf in the pack and then following its movements using a tracking device.

Unlike the grey wolf, all other species of wolves are confined to single continents. The red wolf has met a demise similar to, but worse than, that of its close relative the grey wolf, and its true type now exists in the wild only as a reintroduced population in North Carolina, whereas its range once took in part of Texas and all of Florida. In the 1700s and 1800s people reported encounters with these cinnamon-coloured to tawny-coloured wolves. Red wolves were hunted relentlessly and also poisoned by the early European settlers, who thought the wolves killed domestic animals and also humans. Added to this destructive force was the invasion of coyotes who moved in once the settlers expanded their agricultural lands and interbred with the red wolf. In the 1970s, when the last wild red wolves were about to disappear altogether, some were captured for a breeding program aimed at, eventually, reintroducing the species to the wild. Many were caught and examined and, from these, fourteen considered to represent the true breed of red wolves were selected for the breeding program. The captive breeding program has been very successful, resulting in several hundred red wolves. Some of the offspring of these animals have been released into areas where they will not interbreed with coyotes, including islands off Carolina and Mississippi and one site in North Carolina. It remains to be seen how they will survive.

The Ethiopian wolf, also known as the Simien jackal, is considered to be the most endangered canid of all. Just over one hundred years ago they occurred throughout Ethiopia. Now only six populations of them exist, in the highlands of Ethiopia at altitudes between 3000 and 4000 metres, and these have a total of no more than 500 individuals. For many years they have been hunted and killed by humans and their habitat has been destroyed by the expansion of agriculture. This has either driven them to the mountains away from humans or meant that only those always living in the mountainous regions have survived. The main reason given for shooting them is that they prey on sheep but this is incorrect. The Ethiopian wolf feeds mainly on small rodents. Human contact has forced them to carry out more of their hunting and other activities in the night. In other words, they have shifted from being primarily diurnal (active during the day) to nocturnal (active at night).

Examination of the DNA of the Ethiopian wolf suggests that the species is more closely related to the grey wolf and even to the coyote than to any of the canids of Africa. This makes these animals unique in their own environment. But this status is under threat since the remaining members of the species are beginning to breed with domestic dogs and, if this continues, their uniqueness will, to a large extent, be undermined.

Another canid referred to as a wolf is the maned wolf, which belongs to a different genus than the other wolves. In fact, this species is more closely related to foxes than wolves. It has a beautiful red coat, like the red fox, but much longer legs. Unlike the grey wolf, the maned wolf is not a pack-living animal. Its more solitary life is closer to that of foxes. The species is found in South America, in Bolivia, Uruguay, Brazil and Argentina, where it is hunted by those fearing that it will kill their livestock. There is little evidence that such fear is based on fact. The maned wolf's preferred diet is small rodents and birds.

The coyote, also known as the prairie wolf or brush wolf, occurs throughout North America and as far south as Central America. This range is extensive and varied both in terms of climatic conditions and types of vegetation. Its dens can be found from bushy slopes to rocky ledges. The coyote has been unusually successful in expanding its distribution and numbers over the last one hundred years, possibly as a result of a declining number of wolves. Its population size is estimated to be 7 million and its outer range has moved as far north as Alaska and South to the Yukon and Central America. Some forty to seventy years ago, coyotes became established in the north-east of the United States and from there expanded north to Nova Scotia. Then, around only forty years ago, the species spread south as far as western Panama, and also into Mississippi and Florida. Their colonisation of new regions has gone hand in hand with their ability to accept a wide variety of prey and to eat fruit, and even grass, when conditions demand it. These abilities have served them well for survival even though they have been hunted and killed by farmers. Some believe that slaughter by farmers has forced the coyote to become nocturnal. Hunting by stealth in darkness, the coyote covers around 4 kilometres a night.

It is thought that humans have assisted the expansion of the coyote by reducing the numbers of grey wolves, a natural competitor, although some of them actually interbreed with the grey wolf. We may also have assisted their spreading into new areas by clearing parts of forests.

Each pack of coyotes has a home range, or territory, to which it adheres quite faithfully but some coyotes are transient. The latter are the non-breeding, young, old or disabled coyotes. A breeding pair is always resident in a stable home range. The size of the home range varies greatly from place to place, and may be from 10 to 100 square kilometres in area. In some places the same home range is shared by both the adult males and female and in other places, it seems, the male has a larger range than the female. This depends on the availability of food and other conditions of their habitat. The social groupings of coyotes also vary with these conditions. In poorer conditions, coyotes live as male–female pairs but, in more favourable conditions, they stay together in larger groups, although they are less social than the grey wolf. This might explain why numbers of coyotes have increased while those of the grey wolf have declined—coyotes can hunt, reproduce and carry out other activities necessary for survival in small groups and pairs but wolves need larger groups to do so.

Foxes

Foxes inhabit all five continents of the world (Figure 2.2). A greater variety of species called foxes is present in the Southern Hemisphere than in the Northern Hemisphere, where the distributions of species are more continuous and overlapping. The red fox is the most widely distributed member of the Canidae. Its range covers almost all of Asia and Europe, and it is also present in parts of northern Africa and North America.

The home range of individuals varies from 20 square kilometres, in places where food is scarce, to as little as 0.1 square kilometre, in places where food is abundant. The latter applies to many suburban areas, where foxes may live in close proximity to humans. In Europe the number of red foxes is increasing, in contrast to the declining numbers of the grey wolf. As the wolf dies out, the red fox moves into its place. Some say that foxes survive where wolves cannot because they are less social than wolves. They live more solitary lives and they hunt and scavenge for food on their own. The foxes are also very adaptable. They even steal into the centres of European cities at night to feed on food waste or rodents.

The natural range of the red fox does not reach the tropical regions and its only presence in the Southern Hemisphere is in Australia and some of the Pacific Islands. Europeans introduced it to Australia in the 1840s as prey for the so-called sport of fox hunting. Further releases occurred in Australia in the 1870s in an attempt to curb the spread of rabbits, which arrived with the first settlers. Once in Australia, the red fox was quick to adapt to new environments and became widespread. It now inhabits all areas of mainland Australia, except the tropical northern regions. The rabbits assisted this process. Spread of the rabbits, often in plague proportions, was

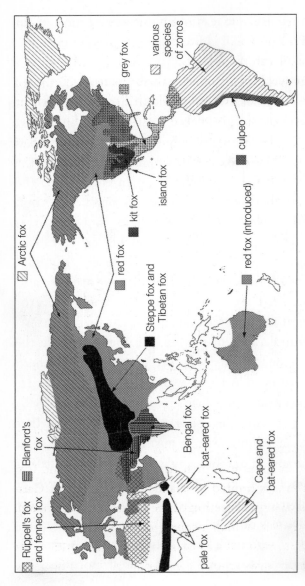

Figure 2.2: Distribution of foxes.

The approximate current distributions of the foxes, which cover all five continents, are shown. Note that the red fox was introduced to Australia. The zorros are the foxes of South America. There are six species of zorros, each with its own distribution but shown collectively here. Only one species of culpeo exists. To simplify the shading, the distributions of Rüppell's fox and the fennec fox are shown together, and the Steppe fox and the Tibetan fox are also shown together. Note, however, that these are four separate species.

followed by spread of the foxes, taking advantage of this readily available food source.

Although the range of the red fox extends into the Arctic Circle, this is primarily the domain of the Arctic fox. This species circles the North Pole, occurring in northern Asia and Europe, Greenland, Iceland, northern Canada and numerous islands. It is the only canid that can survive in these extremely cold climates. Their fur is very thick and covers their feet to protect them from frostbite. Their ears and snout are also less vulnerable to frostbite because they are relatively smaller than those of other members of the Canidae.

The grey fox is also known as the tree-climbing fox because it does, in fact, climb to safety in trees. To do so the fox gains a footing using the long claws of it hind feet and reaches up with its front feet. Once the danger has passed it descends from the tree backwards. The distribution of this species extends throughout the United States and into parts of northern Canada. In the south it occurs throughout Central America and into Columbia and Venezuela. Grey foxes live in a range of different habitats, even close to cities. The species is killed in large numbers to meet a growing demand for its fur.

The other foxes in North America are the island fox, whose habitat is limited to islands off the coast of California and to a small section of the Californian mainland, and the kit fox, which occurs in the western United States. Island populations of any species are vulnerable and this is certainly true of the island grey fox. The home range of these foxes is only half a square kilometre and up to seven individuals may inhabit an area this size. This is amongst the highest population densities recorded for canids. Such dense populations lose genetic variability and become at risk of being wiped out by a change in climate and food availability or by disease. They are less adaptable than more widely dispersed populations with greater variability in habitat occupation and a wider range of other characteristics.

The kit fox is often also called the swift fox or the prairie fox but others argue that swift and kit foxes should be recognised as being separate species. These foxes live on opposite sides of the Rocky Mountains and seem to make up two distinct genetic populations. Both the kit and island foxes are at risk, because of their confined populations, and attempts are being made to ensure their survival.

Foxes, or zorros, are found throughout South America. The crab-eating zorro is present in open forest areas of Brazil, Columbia, Venezuela and some neighbouring countries. It covers regions also inhabited by the maned wolf. The culpeo, or Santa Helena zorro, occurs along the western side of the continent and up to high altitudes in the Andes. Very little is known about the ecology of the other foxes: the grey zorro (also known as the Argentine grey fox or chilla), which is sought after for its fur; the pampas fox (or Azara's zorro); the small-eared zorro; the Sechuran fox or zorro and the hoary zorro (or small-toothed dog).

Off the coast of Chile is Chiloe Island, where Darwin's fox—named because Charles Darwin was the first to describe it scientifically—lives in temperate rainforest. Only about 500 of these foxes remain on the island but recently another population of them has been discovered on the mainland. This suggests that they were once more widespread and now only pockets of the original population survive.

Africa has five fox species. The bat-eared fox (also known as the black-eared or Delande's fox) has two distributions: one on the eastern side of the continent from Somalia to Tanzania, and the other in the south, from Angolia and Zambia to the Cape. In the past, these two populations must have been one continuous, inter-breeding population. The distribution of the Cape fox (also known as the kama fox or silver jackal) overlaps that of the bat-eared fox in the southern Cape region. The pale fox (also known as the pallid or African sand fox) is an inhabitant of the arid regions bordering the Sahara on its southern side, whereas the fennec fox and Rüppell's fox (or sand fox) cover the arid regions to the Sahara and across North Africa into the Middle East and as far as Afghanistan.

Finally, there are the foxes of Asia and the Middle East, beginning with Blanford's fox, also known as the Afghan or hoary fox. This species is found in Afghanistan and surrounding regions extending westward into Israel, where it is protected. It is most numerous in Israel and rare in all other parts of its range, where it has no protection. It is a small fox inhabiting high altitudes and with large ears like other foxes living in arid zones. Next there is the Bengal or Indian fox, present throughout India and also in open areas in Nepal and Pakistan. They are killed relentlessly for sport but, nevertheless, seem to be surviving relatively well. The Steppe fox, also called the Corsac fox, has a large area of distribution over Central Asia. This species is notably more social than the other foxes and inhabits large labyrinthine burrows. The highland Tibetan fox is limited to Tibet and a small part of Nepal and India. They are shy of humans, and for good reason because Tibetans favour their fur to make hats.

Jackals

Jackals occur in Africa, the Middle East and Asia (Figure 2.1). The side-striped jackal is found only in Africa, where it inhabits the mid-region, which is tropical. It is wide-spread but because it is rare and quite secretive it is usually only seen in national parks. The golden jackal, or Asiatic jackal, has a much larger distribution, from North Africa to Thailand. The record of its fossils suggests that the golden jackal evolved somewhere outside of Africa and then spread into Africa about 500 000 years ago. Golden jackals prefer dry open country. Unlike the side-striped jackal, this species does not fear humans greatly and they will live near villages and cities. In fact, its scavenging activities around villages serve to clean up garbage, as well as rats and mice. The Ancient Egyptians immortalised the species by using the golden jackal form for the god of the dead, Anubis. Apparently, even today golden jackals are quite common throughout their range.

The black-backed jackal, or silver-backed jackal, occurs only in Africa in two separate populations, as does the bat-eared fox and, surprisingly, in similar regions. One population occurs in the north-east of Africa and the other in the south. Black-backed jackals are highly carnivorous. They are hunters as well as scavengers. They are, themselves, also hunted, both by farmers, who want to protect their flocks, and by birds of prey. The birds of prey take the jackals when they are young.

Dogs

African wild dogs (also known as the Cape hunting, African hunting or African painted dog) are sparsely dispersed over their entire range. They used to inhabit almost all the continent of Africa south of the Sahara desert. Now their range does not extend further south than the northern parts of South Africa, including the well-known Krüger National Park, and it goes no further north than a belt on the southern edge of the Sahara, with small populations to the north in Ethiopia and in the Sudan (Figure 2.3). Although this range may sound as if it is still quite extensive, their numbers are very low and the populations are highly fragmented even though African wild dogs traverse wide distances in search of food, mates and new territories. The males disperse over

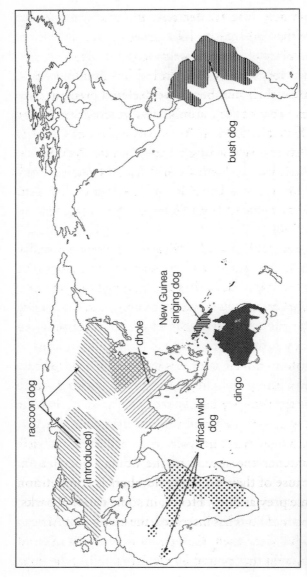

Figure 2.3: Distribution of dogs and dingoes.

The approximate distributions of the species referred to as dogs are shown. The dhole is also known as the Asiatic wild dog. The raccoon dog has two separate regional distributions: one is its original range including south-eastern Siberia, China and Japan, and the other is its introduced range in western parts of the former USSR and Europe. The singing dog of New Guinea is semi-feral rather than entirely wild. The distribution of the Australian dingo is also shown.

greater distances than the females, and a dog may range over more than 500 square kilometres.

The number of African wild dogs in eastern Africa has declined very rapidly over the last one hundred years. In some areas their numbers have declined precipitously to only 1 per cent of their number five years earlier. Sadly, it seems that only about 4000 or 5000 wild dogs are left in all of Africa. According to the *Lycaon* Population Viability Analysis of Joshua Ginsberg in 1992, even the Krüger National Park has only about 400 wild dogs left. They had disappeared from Serengeti National Park by the early 1990s.

Today the pack size of African wild dogs is usually six to fifteen individuals and packs of more than about thirty dogs are rare. This is in sharp contrast to a hundred years ago, when reports of packs of up to 500 dogs were seen and it was common to find packs of about one hundred individuals.

The decline in their numbers has been attributed to a number of causes, including killing by humans even in regions where they are legally protected, loss of habitat due to the spread of agriculture, declining numbers of ungulates, which are their main prey, and disease. Their decline matches the spread of the human population. Another cause of their declining numbers is competition for the same prey as lions. Hence, in some national parks, as the number of lions has increased, the number of African wild dogs has decreased. Competition of the same kind also occurs with the spotted hyena. In addition, the lions reduce the number of wild dogs by preying on both the pups and the adults.

Since larger packs of dogs are able to hunt more successfully than smaller ones, declining numbers plunge the dogs into near starvation and ill health. Under such pressures, fewer, if any, of the pups survive. In addition, as their numbers decrease, inbreeding may increase, resulting in a decrease in genetic variability and so putting the species at even greater risk of extinction if climatic conditions change or disease strikes.

The African wild dog is now on the list of endangered species but, regrettably, the protection that this affords them may have come too late to save many of the now isolated groups in which pack size is low and living is harsh. Moreover, the dogs still roam outside protected parks and enter areas where they are often shot, despite their protected status.

The Asiatic wild dog or dhole, also known as the whistling hunter, is found in India, throughout South-East Asia and as far as China and Malaysia (Figure 2.3). The dhole is even found on the tropical islands of Sumatra and Java but its status outside India is largely unknown. They are not particularly common, even in India, probably because they succumb to rabies and distemper but also because they take poison baits laid in their range. However, they are often seen in Periyar and Bandipur wildlife reserves in South India, as we had the first-hand privilege of finding out.

The bush dog of South America occurs in the northern two-thirds of the continent where there are neotropical rainforests. In appearance, they are quite unlike the other wild dogs, with a long body, short legs and small ears, but it is said that ones reared as pets by the local Indians behave like domestic dogs. They hunt in water and are strong swimmers. Sighting them in the wild is rare.

The raccoon dog, as its name implies, could be mistaken for a raccoon. Its facial markings are like those of the raccoon with the distinctive dark markings around the eyes. The legs are short, ears small and body quite sturdy. Originally an Asian species found in China and Japan, raccoon dogs were introduced to the former USSR and spread west, both of their own accord and by various releasing programs, to Scandinavia and through Europe to France. Their successes in Europe, however, are not matched in Japan, where they are hunted and killed to such an extent that their numbers are declining.

New Guinea singing dogs and dingoes

The Australian dingo once occurred throughout the mainland (not in Tasmania), having reached that part of the world from South-East Asia. It seems that dingoes first appeared in South-East Asia about 100 000 years ago and were taken to Australia probably about 4000 or 5000 years ago by the early human settlers, who may have used them as food and for hunting. In fact, dingoes have many characteristics similar to those of the present-day dingoes in South-East Asia, the singing dogs of New Guinea, and even the dogs of earliest human inhabitants of the Americas. Their similarities to the dogs of South-East Asia and New Guinea likely reflect their common origins. Their similarity to the early dogs of the Americas, by contrast, appears to stem from the fact that some sort of selection processes took place naturally and with similar outcomes in each population. These dogs were not bred selectively by humans but humans almost certainly had an impact on which types of dog survived and which did not.

European settlers in Australia poisoned and shot the dingo as it competed with their farming practices and this continues today. Australian dingoes are now absent or uncommon south of a dog-proof fence, which extends from the north-eastern tip of New South Wales, through southern Queensland and across South Australia. They are also absent in an area skirting around Perth in Western Australia. Elsewhere the dingo is quite common, especially in the northern regions of Australia. Pure dingoes are found in the north but in south-eastern Australia, where feral domestic dogs are common, many are hybrids with domestic dogs. It is estimated that only just over half the wild dogs in south-eastern Australia are pure dingoes.

THREE

The Indian dhole,
Cuon alpinus,
with all senses alert.

Sensory abilities

Wild dogs make use of all of the five senses: seeing, hearing, smelling, tasting and touching, to differing extents depending on their lifestyle and what they are doing at any particular time. Their olfactory (smelling) and auditory (hearing) senses are particularly acute and better than those of humans.

Seeing

Mammals active at night (nocturnal) and those active during the day (diurnal) have different kinds of vision. Colour vision is most useful during the day, whereas at night, sensitivity to very low levels of light is more important. Hence, species that are purely nocturnal have a different numerical combination of the two types of light sensitive cells (called photoreceptors) in the retina of their eye than diurnal species. They have fewer of the photoreceptors called 'cones' that respond to colour and fine details of the objects seen; and more photoreceptors called 'rods' that detect low levels of light and respond to movement.

Although some canids are more nocturnal and others more diurnal, most are active at some time during both the night and the day. This means that they have to be able to see under two very different conditions. In general, they can do this by making a compromise, because their ability to see colour and fine detail is weaker than, for example, humans, but their ability to see at low levels of light is better. They also have a special structure at the back of their retina that enables their eye to collect as much light as possible. This structure, called the 'tapetum lucidum', is a mirror-like cup around the back of the eye and it is the reason why, at night, the dog's eyes reflect brightly when one shines a torch or spotlight at them. The tapetum lucidum collects any light rays that have passed through the retina without stimulating photo-receptors and shines them back, so providing the photoreceptors with a second chance to respond. This means that vision is possible in very dim light. The cost of doing this is a reduced ability to see fine details because the light reflected back from the tapetum is scattered and, in effect, the image is slightly blurred.

The cone cells in the retina allow us to see colour because they have different photopigments that absorb different ranges of wavelengths of light. Humans have three photopigments, but dogs, like many other mammals, have only two. We refer to their colour vision as being dichromatic, compared to trichromatic in humans. Being dichromatic allows dogs to see colour but not to the same degree that we do. They are like colour-blind humans, who can see colour but not all the colours seen by most humans. Domestic dogs are known to have colour pigments in their cone cells that would allow them to distinguish bluish-violet colours from colours in the greenish to yellow-red range but they cannot distinguish within each of these colour ranges. Of course, the dog may not perceive the colours it sees as we do, but it does mean that dogs are not able to tell the colours of traffic lights and, like red–green colour-blind people, must learn which is which by position. They are able to tell whether the top, middle or bottom light is on because that light will appear brighter but not coloured. Probably there has been no demand for wild canids to discriminate these colours and the colours that they can see serve them well enough in their particular habitats.

As the only information we have so far on colour vision in dogs comes from studies of the domestic dog, we cannot exclude the possibility that there may be some differences from one genus of wild dog to another. While it is most unlikely that any of the canid species has more than two photopigments, it is certainly possible that differences occur in the types of pigment, and that would alter exactly what colours they see.

A study carried out many years ago showed that domestic dogs can recognise an object better when it is moving than when it is stationary. Their inability to clearly distinguish colour is counterbalanced by a superior ability to see movement, as is the case in colour-blind humans. Detection of movement is excellent in the African wild dog and the wolf species, and they use it when hunting. As well as an ability to see shades of grey and movement, dogs must have a wide field of vision. The dog's eyes are positioned slightly to the sides of its head so that there is a wide field of vision but not to the extent that there is no longer a reasonably good overlap of the visual fields of both eyes in front. This overlapping field of vision, known as the 'binocular field', allows the dog to have good perception of the distance at which different objects are located. The brain is able to then compare the slightly different images seen by each eye and use this to compute distance in the binocular field. There are other ways of seeing depth but this way is special. In other words, canids have good perception of depth in the binocular area and this ability is well used in hunting. But, at the same time the hunting dog needs to compute the distance of its prey, it needs to keep an eye on the other members of its hunting pack, and also on other members of the same herd as its quarry. This is where having a wide angle of vision pays off. In fact, if you drew a circle around the dog's head, and in the horizontal plane, you would find that the dog can see over about three-quarters of that circle. Only the quarter of the circle behind the head is a blind area. By contrast we see less than a third of the way around the circle.

Near objects versus distant ones are brought into focus on the retina, so that they can be seen clearly, by changing the curvature of the lens in the eye. Dogs have a more limited ability than do most humans to change the curvature of the lens, which means that, when they get very close to objects (30 to 50 centimetres from their eyes), they may not see them at all clearly. At such distances, sense of smell must become more important than vision. At least, we know this is the case for domestic dogs but we have little evidence of the same in wild canids.

Although some breeds of domestic dogs have a propensity for short-sightedness, which means that they cannot see well at a distance, this is not true for breeds used as working dogs and it is most unlikely to be true of wild canids. Good distance vision is essential for successful hunting for food.

Successful hunting in wild canids is also achieved by a special feature in the centre of the retina, which allows them to examine the horizon very clearly. It is an area where special cells called 'ganglion cells' are packed more tightly together and, as a result, images falling on this part of the retina are seen in more detail—that is, with greater acuity. In the human retina, the ganglion cells are in higher density in a small, circular area in the centre of the retina, known as the 'fovea'. This is the area of the retina that we use when we are reading. In canids the area of higher density of ganglion cells is in the centre of the retina but it is a long streak stretching horizontally across almost all the retina. This is a benefit in hunting large prey in open terrain because their images appear along the visual horizon.

Hence, canids have many visual adaptations that suit their vision to their lifestyle in general. The parts of the brain that process this visual information must also be adapted to match the specialisations of the dog's retina and other structures of its eye but these have barely been investigated in dogs so far.

Hearing

The dog's ears, as we see and refer to them, are really ear flaps, called 'pinnae', and they are used to collect sound waves that are then sensed by the hearing organs inside the head. Two characteristics of the pinnae are important for hearing. The first is their size and the second is the ability of the dog to move them to face different directions. Larger pinnae are more effective than smaller ones in trapping sound. The African wild dog has large pinnae, which it uses in conjunction with its acute vision during hunting. The fennec fox has pinnae that almost dwarf its face, as does the bat-eared fox. These particularly large sound-capturing structures help them to detect sounds made by their prey: termites and beetles, and—less often in the case of the bat-eared fox—small desert rodents. It is not uncommon to see a fennec or bat-eared fox looking intently at a spot on the ground while it rotates its head from side to side. It is doing this so that it can pinpoint the location of its prey, hidden underground or in a tuft of grass and making small sounds as it moves around or vocalises.

But large ear flaps serve another function in addition to their role in hearing. They have many blood vessels close to the skin and so act as a cooling device by allowing heat from the body to be dissipated. Hence, it is not uncommon for desert-dwelling mammals to have large ears. This is true of hares, compared to rabbits, and donkeys, compared to horses. It is also the case for canids: those species inhabiting hot climates have larger pinnae. This is a second reason why the pinnae are large in the African wild dog, fennec fox and bat-eared fox. Canids living in cold climates need to minimise heat loss and so they have much smaller pinnae. For example, the Arctic fox has very small pinnae and, when this fox has its thick white winter coat, its pinnae are well covered by hair to protect them from frostbite.

A dog can move its pinnae independently to scan for particular sounds. Then, once the dog has detected a sound that captures its interest, it turns both pinnae to face the source of the sound. By moving its pinnae it is able to detect sounds coming from behind, as well as from the side and in front. Moveable pinnae make hearing very sensitive but quite complicated. The brain has to compute where the pinnae are turned, and assess each one independently, in order to determine the location of the source of a sound. Dogs have evolved the nerve cell circuitry in the brain necessary to analyse this complex information.

Dogs can hear much higher pitched sounds than can humans. This means that they can hear ultrasonic sounds. Humans can hear sounds of up to a frequency of 20 kiloHertz (a measure which indicates the number of cycles of the sound wave per second), whereas the red fox hears up to 65 kiloHertz and the coyote up to a remarkable 80 kiloHertz. To illustrate what this means, let us consider the notes on the piano keyboard. Humans can hear up to about twenty-eight additional keys above the highest-pitched note of the keyboard (that is, on the right-hand end of the piano), whereas the red fox can hear up to forty-eight keys above the highest-pitched note and the coyote can hear up to about double that number of extra keys. This range of hearing would be equivalent to having almost another two entire keyboards attached to the right-hand end of the piano.

What use do they make of this remarkable ability? Since many small rodents and insects communicate with each other using ultrasonic sounds, the ability of canids to hear ultrasound must be helpful in locating these types of prey.

The pitch discrimination of dogs is also quite remarkable. They are able to discriminate notes that are only one-eighth of a tone different in pitch. They probably use this special ability when they communicate with each other using vocal signals.

Smelling

Dogs have an excellent sense of smell (olfaction) and, apart perhaps from hearing, it is the most well developed of all their senses. Dogs are able to detect odours at far lower concentrations than we can, and they are much better than we are in discriminating one odour from another.

Inside the nasal cavity there is a kind of skin with nerve cells specialised to detect airborne scents. It is called the 'olfactory epithelium'. The area of the olfactory epithelium in the dog is about 100 square centimetres, compared to only 5 square centimetres in humans. Added to this, the parts of the brain that process olfactory information are much larger and more complex in dogs than in humans. One consequence of this is that dogs can detect some odours at a million times lower concentration than the lowest concentration that a human can detect.

Not only is a dog able to follow the trail made by a human or other animal but it can also tell in which direction the person or animal was moving. To do so, the dog compares the odour at one part of the trail with that a short distance on, the distance necessary being just two to five footprints of a human. Knowing that the footprints with the most volatile odour will be the later-laid ones, the dog is able to compute the direction in which the person walked. To do this, the dog uses its sensitivity for extremely low concentrations: it must be able to tell when the concentrations differ by only one part in two thousand or so. It is difficult for us to imagine this degree of olfactory sensitivity but we have the same degree of sensitivity in our sense of vision.

The extraordinary sensitivity of the dog to such low concentrations of odours might not be especially useful were it not coupled with another remarkable ability, and that is the ability to single out one odour from a rich background of smells. The dog has to distinguish between competing odours and, to go further, it must be able to recognise a mixture of odours from a common source against a background of others. We know next to nothing about how animals, including humans, recognise mixtures of odours that, for example, may come from one individual and make that individual smell differently from all others.

So powerful is the dog's sense of smell that some anthropologists suggest that early humans came to rely on it quite soon after the lives of dogs and humans became associated. Today we rely on dogs to detect odours that we cannot. For example, dogs are used to sniff out drugs in luggage, detect very small gas leaks in pipelines and even to detect bombs.

Wild canids use their sense of smell for two important purposes: to detect their prey and to recognise other dogs. Scented urine, for example, is used by one dog to send a message to another. By sniffing urine the dog is able to tell the identity of the dog who left the mark and how long ago the urine was deposited in that spot, as well as the dog's sex and, if it is a female's urine, whether or not she is in oestrus (on heat). It is common for one dog to urinate over another dog's deposit of urine, perhaps to mask the scent of the latter. However, dogs have such an excellent ability to discriminate mixtures of odours that they might even be able to distinguish the fact that two individuals have urinated on one spot and even who did so first and second.

Eventually odours in urine dissipate and the sniffing dog can no longer detect them. The rate at which this occurs depends on the particular odour itself and the climatic conditions. In hot dry regions odours must dissipate sooner than in colder regions. Added to this the same urine deposited in an icy cold region might not smell as strongly as in a hot, dry region. Of course, this does not mean that dogs cannot smell urine deposited in snow or on ice, and there is evidence to show that they can. It does, however, make it possible that different species of canids may have different olfactory capabilities to deal with the particular habitats in which they live. It is possible that canid species adapted to living in cold climates are more sensitive to very low concentrations of odours than are those adapted to hot, dry climates, but there has been no research on this topic.

As would be expected, not only do canids have a well-developed sense of smell, but also the ability to produce potent odours from scent glands. These glands are a powerful means of communicating with their fellow species. Other odours that enable dogs to identify members of their pack are those of the mouth and face, which are specific to individuals and are also affected by what the dog has eaten.

Wild dogs use their sense of smell with great sensitivity when they are tracking their prey. They are able to detect the odour tracks of prey long after it has been in an area. It is this ability to recognise a specific odour, or mixture of odours, that domestic dogs use when they track down humans. In fact, experiments have shown that tracker dogs are able to match the odours collected from different parts of the human body; they know that all of the different mixtures of scents from different parts of the body represent the one person, just as we can recognise a familiar person by their hands, back of the head and so on.

Dogs are attracted to the fatty-acid odours given off by rotting meat, which leads them to find, and scavenge, carcasses killed by other carnivores. In the United States one can purchase synthetic lures made of fatty acids and these are used to attract coyotes when surveys of their numbers are being made. The lure draws the coyotes out of cover so that they can be counted. However, if the coyote is trapped and tagged after it has been lured to the odour source, it will soon learn to avoid it. These lures are also used to capture and kill coyotes. Another such lure is a mixture of coyote urine, anal sac secretions and fetid meat.

Added to their ability to detect and recognise odours, dogs form exceptionally accurate and long-lasting memories of odours. Even young pups can recognise their siblings and their mother using smell alone. The mother can also recognise her pups using smell alone, and it is likely that she can tell one pup from another by its odour. One study of domestic dogs has shown that they have remarkable memories of the odour of family members. Pups were separated from their mothers when they were two to three months old and then reared apart. Two years later the mothers were given a choice to approach one of their own pups, now an adult, or another, unrelated dog. The mothers approached their own offspring, showing that they had retained the memory of them over the two or more years apart. Moreover, the brothers and sisters, separated from each other at the same time that they were taken away from their mother, were able to recognise each other. It seems, therefore, that dogs might retain memories of their kin throughout life, and these memories are established before two months of age, possibly even in the first days of the pup's life.

Obviously, this ability to recognise a family member after a long period of absence would be of great importance to the social behaviour of wild canids, since individuals do become separated from their packs or join other packs. Most canid species avoid incestuous matings and they also occasionally sneak away from their own pack to mate with a dog in a neighbouring pack. The ability to recognise a sibling who might have joined the neighbouring pack would ensure that such liaisons are not incestuous. Recognition of family members might also be important in the very positive sense of providing assistance to injured relatives or in assisting a relative to raise her next litter of pups.

The dog's sense of smell, like our own and that of other mammals, changes with changing levels of the sex hormones circulating in its blood. It is well known that females in oestrus or during pregnancy respond differently to odours of food. Their sense of smell is also attuned to odours important for sexual behaviour.

Taste

The dog has a large collection of taste receptors (nerve cells) on the inside of the mouth and on the tongue. Similar to us, they can detect salty, sweet, bitter and sour tastes. This sense of taste is also enhanced by a special organ, known as the 'vomeronasal organ' or the 'organ of Jacobsen', on the roof of the mouth. If the dog licks some urine with the tip of its tongue, it then touches the vomeronasal organ with its tongue and by this means it is able to detect a range of chemicals in the urine. The vomeronasal organ can also be stimulated when the dog touches its upper lip on the urine and then draws its lips back as it lifts its head. This action allows the urine to reach the vomeronasal organ. Called the 'flehmen response', it is seen more often in other species, such as horses, sheep and cats, but it does occur in dogs, especially in coyotes and jackals. 'Urine tasting' is particularly important in detecting whether the female is in oestrus.

Touching

A dog's tactile sense is present at birth, and perhaps even before it. Newborn pups use touch, and probably olfaction or taste too, to locate their mother's nipples and then it stimulates the suckling response. If separated from their mother, the pups cry, swing their heads from side to side and crawl until they contact their mother's body again. In fact, the pup usually keeps swinging its head, nuzzling and crawling until it has made contact with one of her nipples and attached itself to it. Touching their mother is essential for the pups' sense of security. It probably also affects many of the important processes involved in the pups' development.

In fact, touching remains important throughout the dog's life, as owners of domestic dogs know very well. Patting a domestic dog is rewarding to both dog and human. Dogs also use touch in communicating with each other, especially during play and in sexual behaviour. Dogs in a family or a pack also like to sleep touching each other, even if the touch is just a paw on the next dog's back, and closeness is often expressed by sleeping with backs pressed tightly together or the head of one dog resting on the body of another.

The whiskers of the dog are very sensitive to touch. They have special sensory hairs for this purpose, and they are not only on the sides of the dog's muzzle but also over its eyes and under its chin. The whiskers sense texture (roughness versus smoothness) as well as fine touch. Dogs use them to sense objects, food and each other.

Integration of the senses

Animals rarely rely on only one of their senses at a time. Seeing, hearing, touching and smelling are usually integrated but sometimes just seeing and smelling, or seeing and hearing are integrated. Coyotes, for example, will learn to avoid approaching a lure smelling of fatty acid more rapidly if a visual stimulus that they have not seen before is placed near the lure. They attach what they see to what they smell.

Smelling and touch must also be integrated, especially when the dogs are both touching and sniffing each other during social interactions. Inside the den, the tactile, auditory and olfactory senses would be more important than the sense of vision. Outside the den, vision would become more important and tactile sense, perhaps, less important. Hence, time, place and the type of activity in which the dog is involved will determine which senses are used and their relative importance. Nevertheless, hearing and smell are important senses to all canids, both inside and outside the den. One of the rare sightings of the bush dog of South America illustrates this: the observers reported that the short-legged dogs were constantly sniffing the rainforest floor and that this behaviour was interrupted by brief pauses when they pricked their ears to listen for a sudden noise.

The height of the animal itself, or specifically the height of the animal's head above the ground, also determines the use of different senses. Long-legged species can see above grasses that would completely envelop shorter-legged ones. The latter might be forced to rely to a greater extent on hearing and smell in such circumstances, or to adopt different behavioural patterns, such as leaping as they run, in order to catch glimpses of their visual surrounds. We often forget that 'the dog's eye view' of the world differs from ours.

As dogs become old, their vision deteriorates. As we know from domestic dogs, cataracts are a common cause of this but deterioration of the retina also occurs. Age-related deterioration in vision would occur in dogs in the wild too, but only if they live long enough. If so, this would mean that they would have to rely more heavily on their other senses. Although hearing and the sense of smell also deteriorate with increasing age, as studies on domestic dogs indicate, this usually occurs only after vision has deteriorated. One study has shown that the olfactory epithelium (the sensitive skin in the nasal cavity) of domestic dogs does not show any signs of deterioration until after the dog has reached fourteen years of age. Few, if any, canids in the wild are likely to reach this grand old age.

FOUR

Threat display by the grey wolf, *Canis lupus*.

Communication

Animals use signals to communicate. By seeing, hearing, touching, smelling and tasting they are able to perceive, interpret and respond to certain signals sent by other animals. Most animals specialise in the type of senses they use to communicate.

Although all five senses are well developed in canids, acoustic (vocal) and olfactory (odour) signals are the most elaborate ways in which they communicate. For example, wolves can assess odour plumes through a wooded area from as far away as 2 kilometres, and the grey wolf can hear howling over a distance of 11 kilometres. The reliance on these two senses is not surprising since many of the wild canids are active at night when visual signals are less effective. But canids do also use a wide range of visual signals to communicate, and these include facial expressions, body postures and movements of the ears and tail. Communication using the taste and tactile senses is mainly utilised in the social contexts of play and sexual interaction.

Communication in canid society

All mammals need to communicate to regulate mating and to raise their offspring. This aspect of social life requires a certain number of signals. If raising the young is under the regime of a single adult, usually the mother, she needs to be able to communicate to her offspring when to stay at the den and when to follow her. She also needs to be able to respond to the pups' signals of distress and the pups' need to understand when she is displeased. Communication usually becomes more complex when two adults bond to form a pair, and when animals form larger social groups.

Pair-bonding is a form of commitment that requires regular reinforcement. Hence, species that pair-bond tend to have developed greeting rituals and other rituals that reinforce the pair-bond. Greeting in canids includes brushing up against the fur of the other, tail wagging and, as part of the pair-bond ritual, licking of the muzzle. Pair-bonding usually also involves courtship rituals and may entail some rivalry between males. In wolves, in particular, male rivalry is communicated by the ritualised circling of the other, bristling hackles and various degrees of low-frequency growling. This is usually sufficient warning to an interloper to step back but, if two similarly strong and mature wolves should have a serious dispute over status or over a female, fights can break out and become serious clashes, leaving one or both wounded.

Once the partnership has been established, the pair may hunt together and, in doing so, they form a bond for foraging for food. When the pups are born, a parental bond replaces this bond. At least initially, the male now goes out to hunt alone but he brings back food for the female while she is lactating and later will also procure food for the offspring. Although parental behaviour varies slightly between different canid species—in some, the male helps more than in others—the main principles are the same. The family unit needs to be able to interact and somehow communicate its intentions to individual members. On occasions when both parents need to leave the den to hunt, the pups must stay behind and, at such times, there must be a way in which the adults can indicate to them not to follow. If the pups strayed from the den, they would be killed. We do not know exactly how this communication occurs because much of the early communication between mother and pups occurs inside the den. Helpers often stay with pups in larger groups, but foxes or maned wolves sometimes need to leave their pups behind on their own. The natural curiosity of young pups would suggest that they would rather explore or follow the parent than to stay behind, so their staying behind becomes a behaviour that most likely depends on parental instructions.

When a family unit remains together for a season, a year, or even several years, as is the case in wolves, African wild dogs and quite a number of other canid species, we speak of a clan. The commonly used term 'pack' specifically refers to a group hunting together. Wolves (grey and red), dholes, New Guinea singing dogs, Australian dingoes and African wild dogs form medium to large clans from which packs are formed. In African wild dogs the clan may consist of thirty to forty individuals but the packs are only four to seven dogs strong.

To examine communication further we need to look closely at the complexity of the group structure and at the ecological conditions in which the various species live. Bush dogs are found in dense tropical environments but the grey wolf, at home in very cold climates, often roams on open plains and in forests with little undergrowth. We would expect that these vastly different conditions might have led to the evolution of different means of communication. There is also the question of the kind of prey each species seeks. Does it require a group effort to bring down the prey or is the food source better suited to individual foraging? In the former situation, we would expect that additional communication is required so that each individual knows what to do and where the prey is. In the latter case, individuals may even be better off foraging by themselves and developing communication only to ensure that others are keeping their distance.

Communicating over distances

Geographical distances

Most dogs have developed systems of communicating over long and short distances but, in some species, one mode predominates over another. For instance, in South America the maned wolf has developed signals especially for long distances, whereas the bush dog has developed a range of vocal signals that are effective for short distances. This is consistent with the differing habitats that they occupy and the ways in which they forage. Maned wolves are largely solitary and their howls carry over long distances. They are used to keeping other members of their species at bay, meeting only for the courtship season, when long-distance calls help them find an available partner.

By contrast, bush dogs usually live in groups and they often occupy dense bush. Such bush offers many surfaces on which sound waves are reflected in different directions. Moreover, rustling of trees in gusts of winds, water flowing nearby, rain falling on leaves all help to reduce and even 'swallow up' any vocalisations. This is referred to as 'sound attenuation'. Whines, with high frequencies, are more audible than howls in environments with high sound attenuation and this is one of the vocalisations that bush dogs use to stay in touch. If they are further away from each other and visually separated, siren (high-pitched) howls are used.

Since bush dogs forage together, much of their communication has developed for short distances and for close communication amongst each other. They have many short-distance vocalisations, such as barking and extended and repetitive whines, each with their own particular functions. Indeed, bush dogs are surprisingly vocal. They vocalise during the hunt, after the hunt, in friendly or aggressive encounters and in courtship.

Long-distance communication also tends to be vocal rather than visual because, in most canine species, eyesight is not their strongest sense. The other mode of communicating over distance and time is by odour.

Social distances

Communication distance is not only a matter of physical distance but also of social distance. Not all communications in canids are meant to attract another individual from the same, or even another species—the 'come here' variety. It is just as likely that a long-distance communication is designed to *increase* distance, whether by scent marking or by vocalisations. In either case the message may be, 'Stay away' or 'This is my territory'. Wolves (grey and red), coyotes, the maned wolf and the Ethiopian wolf all tend to issue howls and lay scent markings to increase the distance between themselves and others, or between their clan and others.

Distance-decreasing communication also serves members of different social groups (clans). The communications between different clans of bush dogs, African wild dogs or dholes, for instance, tend to be distance-decreasing signals. They scent mark to keep other groups away from their territory but they also have to stay in touch with each other. Generally speaking, therefore, a socially close-knit group of canids must use contact signals more regularly than do more solitary species. In fact, the levels of communication within a group are both more subtle and diversified. They go well beyond signals that are used merely as warnings or threats.

Scent marking

Since the sense of smell is so well developed in canids we would expect that it plays an extremely important role in communication. Indeed, all canids, without exception, use olfactory cues extensively for a wide variety of communication signals. They leave their olfactory messages in snow and sand, on tree stumps and clumps of dirt, even on food remnants and around dens.

Through years of observation and careful records, researchers have gradually pieced together what functions scent marking may fulfil. In general, it can be said that scent marking has a number of main functions. It usually identifies the territory and/or the denning area and, beyond this, may be intended to dissuade a potential intruder from entering that territory (it acts as a threat display). Scent marking is also used as a trail mark to indicate an individual's whereabouts. It is also known to be important in reproduction. It aids long-distance sex recognition, indicating reproductive condition and also revealing whether the alpha female is currently pregnant, as well as expressing social status. It is also thought that certain odours may enable reproductive synchrony of the pair or, in some cases, of all members in the clan.

There are differences in scent marking between species. For example, red foxes mark inedible remnants of food with urine, but this habit does not seem to be widespread amongst canids.

All canids have a number of special glands that produce scents and they use these prudently to scent mark. They have one on the tail (situated on the back of the upper third of the tail and usually marked by a dark spot, triangle or line of hair), one in the anal region and additionally a gland between their toes. Domestic dogs, except Rhodesian ridgebacks, lack the tail gland. In wild canids this gland releases an ambrosial type of scent or, according to some, one similar to the odour of new mown hay, whereas the secretion of the anal gland is rancid to the human nose. The gland between the feet allows canids to leave an odoriferous footprint in addition to a visual footprint.

We do not know much about these glands and how distinct they are since our human sense of smell is nowhere near as sensitive as that of dogs. While we have developed the technology to record and analyse sounds that we cannot hear (infrasound and ultrasound) and light that we cannot see (infrared and ultraviolet), we have no comparably sophisticated technology to record and analyse the range of odours that might be contained in scent marks. We do not know whether canids distinguish between their various scent glands in such a way that a mix of deposits might convey different messages. But, judging by the fact that dogs can recognise a human by his or her odours from different parts of the body, we can assume that they may distinguish between the different odours they produce in the same way.

We do not know whether or not communication by odours is to some extent intentional communication or whether scent marking is a reflex activity, controlled by involuntarily autonomic processes. From observation, we do know, however, that canids use these scent-marking glands regularly and that reproductive condition is also conveyed in the scent marks.

In addition to scent marking by glandular secretions, canids deposit odours in urine and faeces, and they distribute them by scratching.

Interestingly, the scent of solitary species is considerably stronger than that of a group-living species. There is an inverse relationship between intensity of odours and sociability. Among the most odorous canids are the red fox and the coyote. The least-social canids have the strongest tail and anal gland odours. Even their urine and faeces are more pungent than that of group-living canids.

Urine markings comprise an elaborate system of communication. In coyotes, there are a number of forms of urine markings that help to discriminate the age and sex, as well as reproductive status, of the individual. Indeed, most of the canids, chief among them wolves, have a very elaborate system of communicating via odours in the urine that is achieved to a large degree by differences in posture when urinating. One posture is referred to as the raised-leg urination posture. This generally identifies males. Another, a forward-leaning posture, is used only by pups, juveniles and exceptionally by adult males. A squatting posture is almost exclusively used by adult females, and by pups.

The different postures ensure that the urine marks are left in different positions. In squatting, urine is found directly on the ground beneath. In forward-leaning urination, ground marks are left in a lengthwise pattern usually deposited against a small upward slope, and in the raised-leg form of urination scent is deposited on vertical objects.

There are very important functional differences between the raised-leg and the squatting markings. Squatting is associated with the acquisition and possession of food. It may indicate that it is the denning season and even indicate the location of the den. It may help pups to develop and maintain site-specific familiarity and it may serve as a reminder of ownership of site in areas of high intrusion.

Compared to the squatting urination, raised-leg urination is associated with territorial boundaries, travel along established routes, aggression, mate possession, courtship and mating. Frequency of marking is highest when travelling and lowest when hunting.

The posture adopted during urination is not simply dictated by the dog's anatomy. For instance, male lone wolves without territory or partners avoid raised-leg urination and squat instead. Although males usually raise their legs and urinate on vertical surfaces, the purpose of sprinkling a vertical surface is clearly to perform an assertive act and a lone wolf is not in a position to do so. In fact, keeping a low profile by not urinating with the raised leg may lengthen the lone wolf's life. Lone wolves fear packs of their own kind because they are often chased and killed by packs. The greatest threat to a lone wolf is a pack of wolves because they regard him as a trespasser.

Urination can also be a sign of submissive behaviour. Licking of the groin (called the inguinal area) and of the external genitalia elicits urination in neonatal pups up to the age of four weeks. Some domestic dogs retain the habit of urinating when they are handled, and some wild dogs in subordinate positions roll on their backs and urinate when another dog stands over them.

Faeces (or scats) are scented via the anal glands and may also serve as marks of communication when deposited on prominent objects (stumps, snowbanks) and, especially, when found in large concentrations accumulated over several months. There may be repeated or multiple visits to the same site indicating perhaps an important meeting place or a crossing of trails. It is common, for example, for red foxes to mark their territory by depositing faeces on prominent physical structures, such as small mounds of earth or logs.

There are additional forms of olfactory communication, such as double markings, in which case squat and raised-leg urine marks appear together in one location and at frequent intervals. This double marking can be read as a particularly aggressive signal to stay away from the area. The breeding male and female deposit these together and at peak frequency just before the pups are born. At the same time, this type of marking may also advertise the fact that there is a den in the area and that this site will be defended. Hence, trespassing is at the intruder's peril. Double marking is an effective threat display and one that gives lone travellers, or groups, the option to withdraw and disappear without causing a fight.

It has also been suggested that double marking by a pair is not done purely to inform others of their territory and their breeding status but also to promote reproduction itself. Breeding season in wild canids comes only once a year (unlike the case in most domestic dogs) and breeding status needs to be achieved by male and female alike. They need to synchronise their reproductive status, so that the male is able to supply fertile sperm during the brief period of time when the female is receptive. It is thought that the joint urinations by male and female are not just a ritual of pair bonding but, in fact, a means of promoting reproductive synchrony.

Most of the scents have to be renewed at regular intervals as they are exposed to the elements and will, in time, fade. Nevertheless, scent markings as a way of communicating are more permanent than the fleeting characteristic of vocalisations or visual signals or displays.

Vocalisations

In wild canids, vocalisations add to visual and olfactory displays and sometimes substitute for these over long distances, in dense cover or, in the case of visual displays, at night. Vocalisations may, largely, serve emotional reactions and intentions but they may also contain elements of higher cognition and be intentional. If specific signals are employed for specific events and outcomes, they may be intentional, planned and may appeal to others in ways that suggests insight. We can study vocalisations more easily than scent marking, and the work done in this area has been very sophisticated. However, no one has as yet investigated the possibility of sound signals that might contain semantically specific information although, in some species, such as the wolf or the dhole, this cannot be entirely ruled out.

There are four general types of vocalisation used by most mammals and birds. One type consists of approach (distance-decreasing) sounds, such as whines or distress calls; another of withdrawal (distance-increasing) sounds, such as howls; and a third type includes warning signals, such as barks or growls. A fourth category just includes infantile sounds. The latter have evolved to elicit maternal behaviour and some of these, interestingly, resurface in courtship and mating, as is known to be the case in red foxes.

Another subdivision of vocalisations is by the characteristics of sound. Acoustic stimuli are not all of the same value and impact. Instead, acoustic signals may have consistent, and even species independent, effects on the responses of receivers. Humans actually share many of the same responses to sound characteristics as dogs, and other species. For instance, rapid, repeated whistles tend to activate and stimulate motor activity, whereas long whistles with continuous descending fundamental frequency tend to inhibit activity. When we ask a question (requiring an action from someone else), our voice shows an upward trend at the end of a sentence. A pup begging for food is employing quite similar vocal techniques, whining at high frequency. When someone gives an order, the voice goes down at the end of a sentence and inhibits whatever activity has gone on before. Likewise, dominant wolves may issue a short growl at low frequency. Some basic vocalisations have been shown to be situated rather persistently in certain frequency ranges across species and some of the basic sounds, for instance, alarm calls, tend to be understood across species because of their vocal characteristics.

In general, researchers have identified eleven or twelve call-types in the different species of canids and these have been subdivided into approach-eliciting sounds and withdrawal-eliciting sounds. Coyotes give eleven different vocalisations, as far as we have identified, that communicate different types of alarm, threat, submission, greeting and contact maintenance. In grey wolves, there are also eleven sound-types, which are the howl, growl, snarl, woof-bark, growl-moan, moan, whine-moan, whine, whimper, whistle-whimper and yelp. Dholes are unique in being able to emit a specific kind of whistle. The closest sound to the whistle is the coo-coo of the red fox. They use this whistle while pursuing prey and as a contact call to reassemble the group. It is not known yet how the whistle is produced but it is known that individuals produce different whistle calls, and whistle calls vary with age (higher frequency in young than in older dogs) but not with social rank.

Red foxes produce about twenty sound-types that are structurally suited for agonistic (hostile) and contact functions. Researchers found that their vocalisations fluctuated with the seasons and were found to be significantly more common during the winter, the time of mating and dispersal, when foxes move over greater areas.

There has been a strange and persistent belief that barking is common only to domestic dogs and that wild dogs do not bark. Some species may not bark very much and the single sounds may not be classified as barks, as in the dingo; however, in general, it can be said that barking is a widespread sound form in all canids. In wolves, contact between individual family members may take place more often than not at distances of more than 50 metres and brief barks are effective ways to draw attention to oneself. When vocal contact between one group and their neighbours occurs over much longer distances, barking and counter-barking may continue for over an hour at a time.

Even foxes bark. Barking in Arctic foxes is used as long-distance communication. A single bark is expressed when one Arctic fox meets an intruding fox within its own territory. A series of barks (up to fourteen sounds) is expressed at territorial borders. Arctic foxes also use vocal signals for individual recognition of family members and members of neighbouring groups. Grey wolves also recognise individuals by their bark alone.

Sound-types alone may not indicate more or less complexity in communication in canids. Most canids are able to mix some of the eleven or twelve basic sound-types. By this process of 'mixing' they can generate a range of composite sounds such as baying (bark/howl) when discovering a scent, or 'yowling' (yelp/bark) as part of group howls, and these mixed sounds may then provide additional information about the signaller's motivations or emotions. However, foxes tend not to mix sounds as do the more gregarious canids and herein lies an important difference for the extent and subtlety of communication.

In-between steps (or gradations) and transitions between one sound-type and the next can also enrich the entire vocal repertoire and provide opportunities for varieties of meaning and the expression of a range of different moods. So far, this aspect of vocal communication has been analysed only for the grey wolf, but it has been discovered that the number of vocalisations produced by this species is well in excess of eleven. This discovery lays the basis for investigating the existence of very complex communication in grey wolves.

Vocalisations of the grey wolf

The grey wolf has a particularly complex vocal repertoire
with many graded and transitional sounds, a specific class
being those of newborn pups (neonatal).

The earliest sounds made by pups only one day old
are distress calls (yelps or screams) that elicit immediate
responses from the mother. They are harmonic sounds.
Between one and four weeks of age neonatal wolves use
barks, growls and clicks. The fundamental frequencies of
these calls decrease as the pups grow older, meaning that
they become lower in pitch. Infantile sounds of wolves
extend to whines and mews. The yell-whine of pups
develops into howling in adult wolves while all other
infant sounds gradually disappear.

Some researchers have suggested that the rhythms of
sounds made by the pups are more important in eliciting
retrieval by the mother than the sounds themselves. Interestingly, neonatal dogs are either deaf or not responsive
to sounds until they are about two weeks of age. Hearing
is fully developed by day twenty-one after birth, but
vocalisations begin at, or even before, birth and the vocal
repertoire is complete by about four weeks of age.

A very detailed study by Ronald Schassburger established that the sound system of the adult grey wolf falls
into two halves. One half of that repertoire is harmonic
and the other half is noisy. These two halves are linked
and each of them is graded. We can, therefore, speak of
a 'linked bipartite sound system' that is both stereotyped

and graded. The importance of this discovery lies in revealing not just the structure but also the possible functions of sound classes.

The harmonic sounds include certain howls, whine-whimpers and yelps. The noisy part of the repertoire includes barks, howls and growls. The information contained within the harmonic portion of the system is more clear-cut and unambiguous, while that contained within the noisy portion of the system is more elaborate and therefore more expressive of subtle motivational fluctuations. The harmonic system contains the emotional fearful elements. Cries for help and distress calls are harmonic in structure and higher in frequency. These can be seen as emotional responses to events. By contrast, the noisy system in wolves represents the confident, controlled and assertive section of the repertoire. Some subordinate wolves might therefore not express the entire range of the noisy system but, instead, retain some of the vocal characteristics (in frequency and harmonic structure, but not in call-type) of immature canids. Harmonic sounds are used in gestures of appeasement and friendly approaches. Barking in grey wolves belongs to the noisy system and consists of single short sounds, occurring solely within aggressive categories (threat, attack, warning, defence and protest) but dogs have developed as many as two to twelve subunits of individual sounds so that even barking may have complex communicative value.

Within the noisy structure of calls, howling and threat growls are probably the most familiar to us and the most studied. Howling is a vocal feature used particulary by wolves (red, grey and maned) and coyotes. It usually serves to increase distance rather than, as many people once assumed, express loneliness and the desire to attract another wolf (or coyote). It has puzzled researchers that howls are usually performed at low pitch (340 to 360 kiloHertz) because such low frequencies often do not optimise signal propagation. However, it is this frequency range that wild dogs have adopted to convey aggression.

Howling is both a threatening and exposing vocalisation. It threatens other canids not to come near and it can convey information as to the identity of the signallers and their location. This can be a risky strategy unless the individual or group is confident. There are some recognisable variations of howls between species, although they can sometimes be hard to discriminate when they are heard in the natural environment. Red wolves tend to have a flat howl, persisting on average for 75 seconds, and they tend to have lower fundamentals and be of longer duration than the howls of coyotes.

Since wolves of any kind and even coyotes may range over large areas, howling ensures that one clan (or a lone individual) has a way of ascertaining a positional map of the next closest group. Because howling is generally an agonistic signal, it is one sound that all wolves and even those of related species take very seriously. An interesting study of grey wolf pups showed that the pups did not habituate to real howls. They listened to every howl as if it was the first they had ever heard. This clearly suggests that howling is a signal that no one can afford to ignore.

On hearing a clan howl, six responses have been identified: the other group or individual may retreat silently, or retreat but reply; the group may remain silent but not move, or reply but not move; or, more aggressively, respond while silently and stealthily moving closer to the other group. This deceptive strategy is used sometimes when the approaching group is not clear about the strength of the other group and wishes to investigate before attacking. The last and most aggressive option is to approach the other clan while vocalising, a clear sign of a declaration of war. Howling therefore can be used by wolves for either avoidance of another clan or for seeking out another clan they wish to attack.

Another signal that belongs to the noisy range of the wolf's sound system is the threat growl. The relationship of this vocalisation to a food resource has been tested. It was found that the intensity of this threat signal was influenced by the value of the food resource. A research team studied the vocalisations made by hungry and well-fed wolves by introducing an intruder to a food resource that they had claimed as their own. A significant difference was found between hungry and well-fed wolves: hungry wolves made growls that were of longer duration and of higher dominant frequency than did well-fed wolves.

What does the linked bipartite system mean?

The excitement generated by the discoveries of a bipartite system (harmonic versus noisy calls) in grey wolves is based on the finding that it fits so well with studies of other animals in which the association between signal structure and signal function has been explored. Birds, for instance, often use higher and more tonal sounds when frightened and noisier sounds when they are issuing threats.

The existence of graded and transitional sounds may also indicate another condition that Peter Marler and William Hamilton reasoned nearly forty years ago. They observed that many primates, and especially the great apes, show a poorly defined structure of most sound signals. They concluded that this was related to the lifestyle of the primates, as well as their evolutionary position. One key characteristic that they observed to be common to all of the primates with noisy call-structures was that they were socially close-knit, terrestrial or semi-terrestrial, and that they lived in relative isolation from species about their same size and structure. Having identified these ecological facts they then argued that these conditions actually favoured a loosening of the strict species-specific types of calls that many species have developed. Instead, since there is no other species of similar acoustic qualities nearby, they may exploit or risk more sound variations. These variations may then evolve into ways of communicating more elaborate information than could be carried in stereotyped sounds.

Hence, in our opinion, Schassburger is right in assuming that, by analogy, the same principles may apply to the wolf. The social order of wolves is close-knit, so much so that the animal's clan structure and family life have become legendary. Amongst wild dogs, the wolf may well have the most complex social organisation, and this social system is matched by a system of expression that is perhaps one of the most advanced amongst mammals.

Yet there is one very important element missing in these characterisations. We need to look at what we mean by 'complex social organisation' and how this relates to the communication-types used. African wild dogs, dholes and wolves all share complex close-knit groups, yet the grey wolf's communication system is thought, by some researchers, to be more complex. However, the vocal communication of African wild dogs has been classified among the most complex, with eleven vocal classes and eighteen subclasses, as well as twitter, begging cries and rumbles that appear to be unique to this species. One important point to note is that the various forms of communication may need to be seen together—the visual, vocal, olfactory and even tactile—to gain a full picture of the complexity of overall communication. For example, why do African wild dogs have fewer facial expressions than wolves? Although it is possibly a moot point to debate whether wolves or African wild dogs may have a little more or less variation and numbers of signals overall, there are however other important questions to be asked. Why would one close-knit group develop more complex signals than another? And what might this tell us about the characteristics that define the group?

In the case of wild canids, we may define a complex group as one larger than the immediate natal group (male, female and offspring) that may contain individuals born in previous years and some stable members. African wild dogs, wolves, bush dogs and dholes fulfil these criteria. All of the clans or packs in these species vary in size but ties between all members of the clan are very close indeed. Further, they have a dominant breeding (alpha) pair and a reproductive hierarchy. This hierarchy is present in nearly all group-living wild canids.

What is different about grey wolves, as compared to African wild dogs, dholes and bush dogs, is that their social organisation has a *vertical* structure. Wolves have not just an alpha breeding pair, but a full hierarchical system built on structural inequality. There are subordinates who need to show their respect to more senior members of the clan and, because such a vertical social hierarchy exists, communication must become very complex in order to determine the degree and the kind of social interaction between members. In this regard, grey wolves have a social structure more similar to that of the great apes (gorillas and chimpanzees) than to some members of their own kind (such as coyotes).

From studies, therefore, it seems that complex vocal communication is governed by three main criteria: one is the absence of similar species in the vicinity, allowing greater freedom of self-expression; another is stability of group size; and the third and most important reason that is often overlooked is the existence of a social *vertical hierarchy*. It is now possible to say why African wild dogs may not have or need as many facial expressions as wolves. African wild dogs have a 'flat' group structure in which all its members, except for the alpha pair, are equal. This means that their hierarchy is largely determined by reproductive status and there are no other distinguishing reasons for inferior or superior status. Bush dogs equally have a flat structure and lack strong elements of competition within the group. They do not have as many 'scores' to settle and hence may not require a communication system that is as complex as that of the grey wolf. But, since relatively little is known about the vocalisations in the different species of canids, it is too soon to say anything definite on these matters.

Body postures

We know that wild canids are extremely expressive in their body movements and some also in their facial expressions. Special body areas (the genitalia and anal areas) are investigated in greetings and all canids can communicate using their tail, ears and spine (curved up or down). In agonistic encounters they raise their hackles (the hair around the neck and shoulders), move their ears forward, lift their tail up and may use their mouth and voice to give further emphasis to their intentions. We then speak of 'piloerection' of the tail, hackles and hair on the shoulders. Shoulders and hackles often have longer hair and, when raised, they enhance the dog's apparent size during aggressive displays. The dog's tail can be held up and erect, horizontal, drooping or between the legs. It can also be held still or wagged.

The dog's ears can be turned to face forward, sideways or backwards and they can be sleeked down. The ears-forward posture indicates confidence, whereas the sleeked-down position indicates fear and submission. The mouth can go through an entire catalogue of movements: teeth or gums can be exposed to varying degrees and subtle shifts can move expressions of calm to alarm or fear to aggression, merely by the way the lips are pulled back or up. Wild canids, as well as domestic dogs, have an open mouth play-face that, coupled with panting in domestic dogs, is analogous to laughter in humans. Overall, one range of facial expressions is reserved for agonistic encounters and another for fearful expressions (together with ear and tail positions), but significantly fewer facial expressions seem to be available for inviting and loving gestures.

The facial expression used for threat is a frown on the forehead and one of a number of lip positions. Retracting the lips is always associated with either aggression or fear. There is a submissive grin (horizontal retraction of lips) and a defensive grin (with wide gape and horizontal and vertical retraction of lips) and an expression analogous to a smile, but the latter may be seen only in domestic dogs. All other lip positions signal the intention to attack, bite or fight. There is only one friendly display involving the lips and this is the play face. Significantly, in most canid species the play face makes the lip muscles relax so that the lips hang loosely over the teeth. The teeth are often not visible in a play face. Together with a complex set of body movements and auditory signals, a number of messages can be imparted.

Many combinations of body language are used in ritualised displays, which often represent displays of status. The most confident display is the dominance display of the alpha male or female, expressed by a posture of head up, ears up, tail held out and even active stares at a potential competitor or an inferior. The more confident the dog is, the higher it holds its tail. A rounded, inverted U-shaped back with the tail lowered, particularly between the legs, indicates submission. A defensive–aggressive display shows aggressive expression of the face but submissive body postures. Subordinates use either active or passive submission displays and when these are not sufficient they turn into displays of fearful submission.

It is useful to link communication with social structures. One may inform the other and therefore lead to specialised forms of communication. Remarkably, in dog groups, these communication patterns are not just used on the odd occasion but find constant application. Every individual needs to obey the rules of the group and constantly do its part to reinforce them. There are no occasions when one group can walk past another without some form of interaction, be this a full investigation, a casual greeting or a set of affectionate or submissive or agonistic gestures. Wild dogs work very hard and very consistently on their relationships and on maintaining the cohesion of the group. It is not surprising that long-lasting groups such as those of wolves invest considerable time in group etiquette.

FIVE

Social interaction in a pack of black-back jackals, *Canis mesomelas*.

Social life

For the human observer, one of the most endearing characteristics of wild dogs is the extraordinary care with which the parents raise their young. Many bird species have such long-lasting bonds and share parental care of their offspring but this is extremely rare amongst mammals, who commonly have all sorts of group arrangements rather than shared parenthood. Indeed, in many mammalian species, such as elephants, the male has no direct part at all in the upbringing of his progeny. In others, such as ungulates and bovines, the offspring have to be ready and on their feet within an hour of being born. The only other mammals, apart from canids, to have evolved systems of joint parental care are some of the primates and rodents.

Growing pups

Dog pups, wild or domestic, are helpless, defenceless and even blind and deaf at birth. Without the protection of adults around them, they would never reach adulthood. From birth to death, their development can be divided into five relatively distinct periods. The first is the neonatal period (from birth to two weeks). The ears cannot hear yet and the eyes are still closed. Thermoregulation is not fully developed in the first three weeks, meaning that the pups are unable to fully control their body temperature and must rely on the mother to assist in either warming or cooling them. The infant will respond to tactile, thermal, olfactory and gustatory stimuli but, as yet, no auditory or visual responses occur. The end-point of this phase is marked by the infant opening its eyes. The second period is usually referred to as the transition period (two weeks to three weeks), a period in which the infant develops all its senses, is able to keep its own body temperature constant and shows signs of orientating itself. In the third period, lasting from about week three to week twelve, the pups not only react to stimuli but actively explore their immediate environment. This is an important time for them to learn their place in the world and how to socialise with others. At the end of this period they begin to explore the area inside the den. The fourth period starts when they emerge from the den and ends when they reach sexual maturity. Since sexual maturity is reached in different canids at very different times or is actively suppressed by the main breeding pair (alpha pair), this period, starting at about the twelfth week, can extend to twelve months or as much as twenty-four months. The fifth period of the life cycle lasts from onset of sexual maturity to death.

The helplessness of the young has substantial repercussions for the way social life is organised. For wild dogs the act of raising a litter is a major investment of time and effort and a very tense period. Life revolves around the den and its safety and provisioning. In the first three weeks or so, there is a need for very close and constant physical proximity of an adult to ensure that the pups are kept warm. Up until the time the pups begin to leave the den, the mother is almost constantly pinned to the den. Even when the pups emerge after three months, an adult, be it the mother or a guardian dog, usually has to stay with them at all times.

For several months, then, the female cannot hunt and obtain food for herself. Sometimes the pack may bring fresh kills for the female. However, all canids have an ingenious system of food regurgitation. That is, they need not risk having a kill taken from them in transport but, instead, the hunting party consumes the meat and then regurgitates it when safely back in the den. The lactating female will accept such fare and later, when the pups are outside the den and no longer suckling but not yet hunting, regurgitated meals become their staple diet. In this transition, their teeth will grow and slowly their own digestive system has time to develop the enzymes necessary to break down the tough and large proteins in meat.

One interesting part of this way of feeding growing pups is the demand placed on the adults. Adults, often not even the parents, are being asked to give up food that they have *already consumed*. Many vertebrate parents will give up food to feed their young but the act of giving up what has already been eaten is the most extreme form of 'giving' that nature may have devised. It may be that evolution of this trait has led to a psychology of altruism for the sake of the group. There are many stories of dogs that have sacrificed themselves in the defence of their human companions. The degree of devotion and faithfulness essential to raising the young thus extends to the group and, in the case of domestic dogs, to humans. These qualities are among the most valued in dogs and might well have contributed to the strong long-lasting bonds between humans and canids starting tens of thousands of years ago.

Play

The other element that tends to endear dogs to humans is their very obvious sense of play. Adult dogs play with pups and they do so extensively and patiently, even initiating play, not just enduring the pranks of their youngsters, as one can observe in so many mother–infant bonds. The pups also play with each other very extensively, a trait they share with large cats. Adult dholes have been observed to play after feeding on a kill, between hunts (successful or not) and near the den sites with pups.

The young play in the morning and evening and do so amongst each other and with adults. Play between adults can include homosexual and heterosexual mountings. The amount of secretion of the tail gland is known to increase in Arctic foxes after about thirty minutes of having engaged in group play and it is therefore possible that play also bestows olfactory pleasures on other canids.

Social rituals

Greetings and meetings

The den is the focus of canine life for at least a quarter of the year while young pups are being reared. Here groups meet frequently and all activities centre on its maintenance and harmony. This centre is also vulnerable and needs to be defended. Since the young cannot run, adults need to be on their guard at all times to dissuade any possible threats, from snakes or other predators. There is evidence, for example, that leopards will take the pups of Indian dholes. The den also has to be defended from intruders of the dog's own kind. It is not surprising then, that elaborate rituals of greetings and meetings have developed to reaffirm bonds and to be absolutely sure that an approaching adult is not an interloper. Pups run towards returning adults and, instead of paying attention to the inguinal region as they did as infants, they now concentrate on the muzzle. They bite and lick the muzzle to stimulate the adult to regurgitate food.

When adults and juveniles return to the den, the genital and anal areas are presented and investigated during the initial social encounter. The ears, mouth and gland situated on the tail are also closely investigated by conspecifics (members of the same species). In Arctic foxes the tail gland is particularly well developed (being circular and approximately 3 centimetres in diameter). These olfactory investigations are a kind of insurance that no mistake has been made as to the identity of the returning adult. Elevated tails and erect hind limbs are other socio-sexual presentations that function in appeasement or greeting gestures.

Submission

Group protocol also involves forms of approach that are at once recognition as well as confirmation of social status. Merely age class can express social status, and younger canids are expected to show respect to their elders.

In hierarchically structured groups, a first meeting or any subsequent encounter needs to contain a message of the dog's willingness to accept its prescribed station in life. Greeting a superior may require a subordinate resting dog to at least nose-push in the direction of the superior dog if he or she passes at some distance away—very much in the same way as we greet each other in the street when passing. The initiation of the greeting by the inferior is also shared by humans. The greeting is not necessarily returned by the superior but woe upon the inferior if she or he has failed to do so! If one of the alpha dogs is passing by more closely, the resting subordinate dog may have to rise and approach the superior with a range of well-defined gestures. Submission is then seen in the effort of the inferior to attain friendly or harmonious social integration. According to the ethologist Konrad Lorenz, submission behaviour of this kind is related to appeasement behaviour and acts as an innate mechanism to block aggression. It may also involve learning, rather than being entirely innate.

Some submission postures expose the most vulnerable parts of the body, especially those that fall into the killing repertoire of wolves, such as the abdomen. It also formalises non-aggression and so avoids any behaviour that could be read as defensiveness or aggression. Submissive behaviour has no doubt high survival value for a species that can kill and has the capacity to kill its (same species) opponents.

In a sense, submissive behaviour retains many of the qualities of the behaviour that pups show to their parents. Mothers clean and lick the anal and genital regions of pups to stimulate them to urinate and defecate. To achieve this, the pup needs to roll over and expose its abdomen. The first experience of exposing the abdomen is thus pleasurable.

Submission can be active or passive, particularly in wolves. Active submission involves a group ceremony whereby members surround the superior as he or she stands still while they nose-push, lick or gently seize his or her muzzle or face. Active submission is also part of parent–offspring interaction. In this case, there is enthusiastic tail wagging first and movement of the hind area by the offspring, coupled with licking of the mother's muzzle. This is derived from a food-eliciting response. The parent or helper will regurgitate food for the pups once they have asked for it in this way.

Passive submission may involve voluntary immobilisation of an inferior, who lies on its side or half on its back, ears facing backwards and sleeked against the head, with its tail curved between the legs. This can occur in response to genital investigation by a superior. The demonstrated helplessness may also act as a reminder of the stage of development when such a posture was part of the pup's repertoire while it was cared for by the parent.

Submissive gestures work only if the superior dog shows a response that is appropriate and reinforces the submissive behaviour. However, not all rituals end in an appeasing way. While the inferior may wish harmonious integration, the superior may not always respond favourably, particularly in the case of a perceived potential rival, or if the approach is considered insolent. The superior may then fight, warn or threaten the submissive individual. In the latter case, the individual is unlikely to achieve social integration. In some cases, an individual may eventually be forced out of the clan.

Since most canids have alpha males and females, females have their own and very similar forms of maintaining their unique reproductive status in the group. Such a female may eventually force out another female who has reached sexual maturity or may even kill the pups of a subordinate female if she has conceived against the rules. Sometimes, the latter behaviour, observed especially in African wild dogs, may be dictated by necessity. If the available food sources are not sufficient for two litters, the litter of the subordinate has to go.

Non-compliance within a group can lead to outbursts of aggression against an individual. Some of these outbursts are extremely short as discipline is swift and powerful. We have seen an interesting behaviour of this kind in a dingo female. She was the adult breeding female and a young male dingo had walked across her patch without greeting her. She ran over to him and in one very swift action, at lightning speed, she grabbed him by the scruff of his neck and threw him over. The young dog then showed all the appropriate submissive behaviour and she allowed him to display this without further punishment for his transgression. In other cases, the dominant dog may make threatening postures consisting of growls and frowns, slightly bared teeth and a raised tail. This advises the inferior to back off and show proper submissive behaviour. The stare, used also extensively in gorilla society, often functions as a powerful ritualised reminder for compliance.

Most social signals are devised to strengthen the harmony of the group and therefore, generally, no harm will come to its members provided they follow the rules meticulously, hourly and daily. There is, however, often not much room for error. Aggression is related to hierarchy, territoriality, to the defence of young, and also to dispersal patterns.

Social grouping and dispersal

Despite common behavioural traits the social systems among canids are by no means uniform. They range from monogamy in Blanford's fox, to occasional polygamy in red foxes, to social and genetic polyandry (where a female mates with more than one male) in Ethiopian wolves. In many canid species, groups develop from the incorporation of non-dispersing offspring: these may be exclusively female, as in red foxes; of equal sex ratio, as in black-backed jackals; or mainly male, as in African wild dogs. Groups can also form from the addition of incoming animals of either sex or by two single sex groups joining together. There is great variation in all aspects of grouping, even within a species.

There is a tendency for social systems to be associated with size: polyandrous systems are characteristic of the largest canids. This association might arise from body size either directly, or indirectly, via the ecological demands on the species.

The type of social system of canids is also interlinked with sexual behaviour and dispersal. In polygamous species there are early sex-related differences in play and in aggression; whereas in North American canids, who are monogamous, there is little divergence in male and female behaviour. Dispersal is about where the young go when they leave the clan, whether they go at all, how far they go from the natal group and whether they go together or singly, in same sex groups or in mixed sex groups.

The dispersal patterns of the African wild dogs are not fully known to this day but it appears from the latest studies of this endangered species that their dispersal is sex biased. A five-year study conducted in northern Botswana found that males disperse in larger groups and further than females, who are less likely to leave home. As a result of this system, African wild dogs do not mate with close relatives, a risk that is ever present in groups that attach themselves to their natal range.

The South American maned wolf and the crab-eating zorro are both monogamous but they differ in social organisation. The maned wolf is largely solitary. Male and female adult individuals are together only during the breeding season and only for the time the pups are being raised. They do not cooperate in hunting and, when they leave, they leave singly.

In crab-eating zorros, the basic social unit is the pair, as it is with the golden and black-backed jackals, the coyote and the bat-eared fox. Group formation is transitory and is determined by the age of the offspring.

Young crab-eating zorros usually disperse between five months of age to a year. This rare forest-dwelling canid has nevertheless some very special attributes. Although the social group may be transitory, they are highly sociable. They sleep together, travel together, always in single file, and feed communally with minimal aggression. Indeed, the marked lack of aggression at feeding sites is one of the very notable behaviours of this species. When they rest, they do not simply lie next to each other but literally fall into 'heaps', one lying on top of the other. They spend half their waking hours in such heaps. There is no good explanation for this behaviour. It may be a way in which they protect each other from the excessive number of biting insects. They also have an alpha pair but there is no other discernable hierarchy, and they subscribe to extensive greeting ceremonies. Non-breeding offspring stay close to the alpha pair and help care for the pups. Dispersals are only to the edge of the natal territory. Offspring return 'home' frequently and dispersed males also return to their natal group frequently, often to help with the next litter.

The social life of Indian dholes shows close-knit patterns similar to those of zorros and African wild dogs. Dholes are about the size of African wild dogs and their current pack sizes (they might have been larger before they were endangered) are similar to African wild dogs as well. An average pack size is about three to five dholes while clans may be made up of twenty or more individuals. Individuals mature within a year, and they mate between September and February.

The dhole mother has to remain with the pups continuously for fifty-eight days. Unlike other canids, dholes maintain a number of dens at the same time, and some of them are reused from year to year and are expanded. They are each like den cities, with several chambers and entrances. Dholes are also unusual in that they shift den sites frequently and, when the pups are small, they do so at the slightest disturbance. This is probably because dholes live amidst a range of formidable predators, such as tigers and leopards, and, despite their courage and strong group cohesion, the clan is usually nervous when the pups are small. Development and clan integration happens rapidly in this species. Dhole pups grow up so rapidly that the pups are fed on kills even before they are four weeks old. They leave the den when they are between seventy and eighty days old and then almost immediately accompany adults on hunts. By the time they are about fifteen weeks old, the pack takes them directly to a kill and allows them to feed first. If there is not enough food for the pack, the juveniles will have the entire kill to themselves. By seven months of age, the juveniles are recruited to help in hunting and killing. When a large kill has been made, young and adults feed together.

The social nature of canids varies greatly. Some are very gregarious, such as Indian dholes and African wild dogs; others have long-lasting pair-bonds, such as the crab-eating zorros; and some are largely solitary, like the maned wolf. To some extent this is also reflected in their dispersal patterns.

Life of the grey wolf

A lifelong commitment

Grey wolves have strong individual preferences. When two individual grey wolves of the opposite sex meet, they will not necessarily become a pair. Even if they quite like each other, they do not rush into a relationship. Wolves pair for life and they prepare for this commitment, as do lifelong pair-bonding birds, by extensive and lengthy courtship rituals. The courtship involves hunting together, intimate exchanges, including caresses, and also extensive scent-marking activities. In exposing scents to each other, as is the case in double-marked urination in particular, male and female wolves become gradually synchronised physiologically and behaviourally for reproduction. Since there is only one breeding cycle in wild canids per year (see Chapter 6), not only does the female need to come into oestrus but the male also needs to produce his appropriate hormones for sperm production and mating. After stimulation towards mating is achieved by these visual and, especially, olfactory signals, the pair chooses a den site and, from the point of mating, this site becomes the centre of the pair's territory. Dens are defended vigorously and uncompromisingly.

When the pair finally gets to mate, they continue the double-scent marking. In fact, the number of double markings are highest after the pair has mated. In the case of grey wolves there are several reasons for this practice. First, if the couple is on its own, the increased double marking serves to warn other wolves that they are breeding and therefore likely to defend vigorously any intrusion into their territory and, especially, any incursions into the area of the den. Second, if the couple is not mating for the first time and is the established pair of a group, the same rituals precede mating but there is one difference: other members of the clan need to know and respect that the alpha pair is breeding. The social hierarchy of the clan demands that usually only the alpha female will reproduce. The rest of the clan, all subordinates, may need to be reminded of this special status and may be intimidated by the double form of scent marking. Third, the continued double marking after impregnation could actively serve to suppress oestrus in subordinate females. The latter possibility is not necessarily shared by other wild dog species. In the African wild dog, for instance, the continued advertising of the reproductive status of the alpha pair may actively *induce* phantom pregnancies in subordinate females. These phantom pregnancies serve a vital function. The subordinate females begin to lactate when the alpha pups are born and the subordinates can therefore function as helpers and nursemaids. It is also an insurance for the clan as a whole. Should an alpha female be killed, the offspring of the pack can then be cared for by the lactating subordinates.

The mating system does not always function as perfectly as this and, sometimes, subordinate females also get impregnated. The chances for their offspring are not very good. They will automatically slip to the lowest rung of the social group and there are usually no males (including the father) or other helpers prepared to assist the subordinate female in raising her pups. Indeed, the alpha female both in wolves and in African wild dogs may eventually kill the offspring of her subordinate.

Maintaining the social fabric

Wolf life is complicated not just by group size and hunting dependence but also by the hierarchical organisation of the group. A colony of birds or a large herd of ungulates ultimately can contend with fewer rules as long as the organisational structure is flat. Also, in a harem of seals there will only be one male who dominates and rules the entire harem. All of the female seals in the harem are equals. Similarly, large colonies of birds usually do not have an overseer. Every bird-pair rules over its tiny nesting space and everybody else is friend as much as foe. The advantage of nesting together lies in a greater chance of survival of offspring. The social life, however, of most wild canids, and that of the great apes, gorillas and chimpanzees, and humans, is strongly hierarchical.

It is this hierarchy that demands constant work and communication of intentions, as well as ongoing reassurance by all members that they accept the rules of the clan hierarchy. The dominant male wolf needs to insist on displays of loyalty and submissiveness if he does not want to lose his position to a contender. Fights between male wolves, as between young adult chimpanzee males, are frequent and the maintenance of power is dependent on constant vigilance. For instance, the alpha wolf needs to display to all the other watchful members of the pack that he is confident, self-assured and will not accept any nonsense. He needs to show this in every move of his body posture, all day and all night. If he maintains a confident posture, he will not be attacked by subordinate males but any moment of uncertainty is likely to be exploited and he may lose his status and his mating rights with the alpha female.

Adult females also have a separate system of vigilance and hierarchy and the alpha female must do her part, just as the alpha male, to ensure that her position remains unchallenged.

The formalities and constant in-group attentions in wolves may seem exaggerated and, at times, pure luxury. Those wild dogs that can afford to turn their eyes inward towards their group members, as opposed to potential surrounding dangers, may give a hint that they are likely to be in the very privileged position of having few real enemies. African wild dogs cannot quite afford to lavish as much attention on each other's status and its possible concerns. The 'flatter' pack structure in which many elements of competition and rivalry fall away may be proportionate to the demands for survival in harsh conditions.

SIX

Greeting between a mother grey wolf and her offspring.

Sex and
reproduction

Wild canids tend to reach sexual maturity later than do domestic dogs. Domestic dogs usually become sexually mature within their first year of life, whereas wolves, for example, do not mature until they are two years old. This difference may be a result of lifestyle rather than biological differences since a recent study has found that male wolves and domestic dogs living in the same conditions in captivity show all of the hormone changes typical of reaching sexual maturity at the same age. The hormones measured were the androgens, which increase during puberty, and they did so at the same ages in the captive domestic dogs and wolves. But there was one difference: the levels of the androgens cycled with the seasons in the wolves but not in the domestic dogs. This hormone cycling in the wolves reflects the fact that, as in other wild canids, their mating is attuned to one season of the year, and sperm is produced only at this time. This cycling is not affected by living in captivity.

Female wild canids, also, usually come into oestrus only once a year, compared to twice a year in most domestic breeds. In those canids that live where winters are harsh and food is difficult to find, the oestrus period is timed to occur in winter so that the pups are born in spring or early summer. Possibly triggered by changing day-length, this precise timing of oestrus ensures that the pups will be well fed. Ethiopian wolves do not experience the same harsh winters but they time the birth of their pups with the end of the rainy season, when they will be less at risk from problems associated with wet weather and able to take advantage of the time when food is abundant. Some canids do not breed at all in years when conditions would be adverse for the survival of the pups. The Australian dingo, for example, does not breed in years when there are droughts.

Having one single oestrus, and hence one ovulatory cycle, per year is a special characteristic of canids. In most other mammals, failure to conceive at one time of ovulation is followed by other opportunities to conceive. A female canid, however, has only one chance to conceive per year and, when this is missed, she must wait until the next year.

Another special characteristic of reproduction in canids is the adoption of a 'locked' or 'tied' position during mating. The mating pair becomes locked when the bulb of the male's penis enlarges to an extent that prevents it from being withdrawn. Hence, the male and the female are unable to move away from each other. After ejaculation has occurred, the male and female may turn to face outward away from each other but the penis remains inserted. Although mating in African wild dogs takes very little time, presumably to minimise the chances of being killed by a predator, it still involves the tied position. In many canids the tied position can last for a considerable time. In grey wolves it lasts for an hour or two. Although it seems that taking up this posture may possibly assist the transport of the sperm, it may also be a means by which the male ensures that his sperm fertilises the ova since, even if she chooses, the female is prevented from mating with another male until his sperm has reached the ova and fertilised them.

Litter size and sex ratio

As a general rule, the larger species of canids tend to produce more pups per litter than do the smaller species, and the pups in the larger litters are smaller and require more care to be reared. In other mammals this pattern is, generally, the other way round: the smaller ones produce more offspring per litter than the larger ones. Amongst wild dogs, the larger species are the grey fox, with an average of between five and six pups per litter, and the African wild dog, with an average of ten to eleven pups per litter but capable of giving birth to as many as twenty pups per litter. Jackals have only about three pups per litter with a maximum of about six. Red foxes also have an average of three pups per litter and rarely more than seven, although up to twelve pups in a litter has been reported. In general the litter size of most other species of fox is three or four pups. The very small fennec fox has between two and five pups in a litter.

But there are exceptions to this pattern. The maned wolf, for example, is quite large but it has only one to three pups per litter. Incidentally, the number of mammary glands (breasts) and nipples of the female canid varies with the number of pups born in a litter. The maned wolf has only four nipples, which means that all of her one to three pups can suckle at once. Most other canids have between eight and ten nipples but the African wild dog has fourteen nipples, which suffices for her mean litter size of ten to eleven pups but leaves a shortfall in cases when larger litters are born. Being a pup in a large litter may often mean waiting for a nipple, unless another female assists in suckling the pups, which does occur although not always (see p. 114).

Within a species, litter size can vary, which suggests that some factor other than adult body size is important in determining litter size. In fact, some recent evidence shows that the availability of food might be more important than body size in determining the number of pups in a litter. For example, the small Arctic fox, inhabiting regions around the North Pole, has larger litter sizes in regions of its range where food is always readily available; in the regions with plenty of food, some give birth to as many as eighteen pups in a litter, compared to the usual litter size of between five and ten. Their food includes lemmings, fish and sea birds as well as carrion.

Another study, by Eli Geffen and colleagues, conducted in 1996, found that larger canids do not necessarily have smaller pups but, instead, litter size varies with the availability of prey, becoming smaller when the prey is less abundant and larger when it is more abundant. Somehow, the females are able to adjust the size of their litters to match the available food and, hence, the likelihood of successful rearing of the pups.

Age of the female is another important factor affecting litter size, as shown in the dhole. Older females have smaller litter sizes.

It is generally thought that the larger canids give birth to more males than females, for example, dholes give birth to twice as many males as females; however, more evidence on this matter needs to be collected. Species approaching the average size for all canids, it seems, give birth to an almost equal ratio of males to females and both sexes provide equal amounts of help in raising the young. In other species of canids with smaller body size, the sex ratio is biased in favour of females. In these species the males emigrate from their family pack and the females tend to stay on as helpers. The red fox has this kind of social organisation.

Sexual liasions

Those wild dogs that form monogamous pair-bonds include foxes, jackals and coyotes. The female of the breeding pair usually does not mate during the beginning of her breeding period, known as the 'proestrous' period. This period may be quite long and it is a time when the bond between the breeding pair is strengthened. The male stays closer than usual to the female and is especially interested in the odour of her urine and her enlarged vulva. The female often becomes more playful as proestrous advances. The next phase is 'diestrous' and it is during this phase that ovulation occurs and mating takes place.

One canid species that does not adhere strictly to the rule of monogamy is the Ethiopian wolf. Observations indicate that around two-thirds of copulations made by Ethiopian wolves are between the dominant female of one clan and a male in another clan. This seems to be an excellent way to prevent inbreeding, but simply observing copulation to take place does not mean that fertilisation takes place. Other methods are needed to discover whether 'extra-pair fertilisation' does take place, meaning that a female in a pair-bond mates and conceives by a male outside that pair-bond. It is possible to do this by comparing the DNA of pups with that of the mother's partner and other adult males either in her clan or in close proximity. This technique was used to examine the paternity of sixteen offspring of island foxes and the results showed that four of the sixteen had been the outcome of extra-pair mating.

Incest is generally avoided by canids, which ensures genetic diversity and increases the chances of survival of the species. Matings between parent and offspring are known to occur in wolves but they are not common. Once the offspring have become sexually mature, they may well stay within their family clan but they do not breed. A study of grey wolves, in which the DNA of sixteen mated pairs was examined, found little evidence of parent–offspring matings or matings between siblings. This means that the dominant breeding pair in a clan is not made up of closely related individuals and the clan has social rules ensuring that incest is avoided.

About one in ten litters is produced by a female other than the alpha female in a clan of African wild dogs. But it is rare for the pups of such matings to survive beyond a year. In fact, the alpha female has been known to kill pups of other females sired by the alpha male. Sometimes they even kill their own daughters' offspring. The outcome of this infanticide is to remove any competition that may have been faced by the alpha female's offspring and make available extra females on whom the pups can suckle.

Cooperative care of the young

Having a large litter size goes hand in hand with needing help in rearing the litter. In many species fathers and siblings assist the mothers in raising the pups. In the case of grey wolves and African wild dogs there is, usually, only one breeding pair in the clan. These alpha individuals are assisted by their maturing offspring to gather food for the pups and often mind them. These assistants may even rear the pups if they lose their mother when they are just a few weeks old. For example, the grey wolf pack has only one breeding pair but the other females in the pack come into oestrus even though they do not mate and they develop pseudopregnancies. This means that they produce milk and may suckle the pups of the dominant female, especially if she is killed or unable to do so herself for some other reason. The fact that the non-breeding females in the clan have pseudopregnancies at the same time as the dominant female is breeding also means that they show maternal behaviour at the same time as she does. This makes for harmony in the clan and assistance in rearing the pups irrespective of whether they are the females' own offspring.

Timing of breeding

In many canid species, every female in the clan comes into oestrus at the same time. Added to this, even females of neighbouring clans may come into oestrus at the same time. For example, Ethiopian wolves in the Bale Mountains breed between late August to late December but the clans within one subgroup of the population all breed within a period of about two weeks.

Why do members of a clan, and their neighbours, synchronise their oestrus so precisely? Some researchers believe that synchronised breeding in neighbouring clans may be a way of minimising predation of the pups because a predator can consume only so many pups within a certain time, thus leaving some alone during their most vulnerable stages. This might also be a reason for having a large litter size. Others suggest that extra-pair mating in a clan might be reduced by synchronising oestrus since the attention of the dominant breeding male is focused on his own female at the time when other females would lure him away with their special smells and soliciting behaviour. This method of control is not perfect but it may still be important. We have mentioned that the other reason for synchrony of oestrous is to ensure that all females, including the ones that do not breed, show maternal behaviour together, thus creating a protective environment in which the pups of the breeding female can be reared.

Life of the African wild dog

A good deal of research on the African wild dog has been carried out in the Krüger National Park in South Africa. There the dogs usually mate in March, in the autumn, and the pups are born between late May and early June, which is at the beginning of winter. Although the breeding season varies quite a lot in different regions, it tends to take place in the driest time of the year when the dogs' prey has to come to waterholes to drink and can be hunted more easily than at other times of the year. The birth of the pups takes place in a den, as typical for most canids, and they stay there, where they are warm and protected from predators, until they are two months old. For the next month they stay near the den and often return to it for protection from predators and the climate outside. By the time they are three months old the pups are ready to leave the den and move off with the pack.

The alpha female has so many pups in a litter that it would be impossible to rear them without the assistance of the clan. Other members of the clan are needed to defend the pups from predators, which are mainly lions, and to provide food. After feeding on a carcass killed by the pack, some of the non-breeding adults return to the den and, in response to the pups licking their face and lips, they regurgitate semidigested meat on the ground near the pups, who then consume it. They also provide regurgitated food to feed the alpha female and any other dog that has stayed in or near the den to stand guard and care for the pups.

Although the pups are already dining on some regurgitated meat by the time they are only two weeks old they are still dependent on the alpha mother's milk at this age. Feeding meat to the pups not only provides them with an additional source of proteins and minerals but also gives them an opportunity to begin to learn social skills that they will use later in life. As the pups cluster around the meat and tear at opposite corners of the larger pieces they learn about competition and sharing. Later they will make use of these social skills when they feed at carcasses of impala and other ungulates killed by members of their pack. They start hunting for their own food when they are around a year old.

An interesting fact about African wild dogs is that the first time a female reproduces she gives birth to slightly more males than females: for every ten pups born at least six are males. Females that have already had one or more litters produce more daughters. The cause of this change in the sex-ratio at birth appears to be the level of the hormone oestrogen in the mother's blood. It is higher in females breeding for the first time than in those that have already had litters.

African wild dog clans are comprised of more males than females. This probably has little to do with a sex-ratio bias in pups at birth and more to do with young females leaving their family clan when they are one-and-a-half to two-and-a-half years old. They may join another clan, but until they do, they are more vulnerable to predators. Young males may stay in their own pack without breeding all of their lives, which amounts to around ten years. Should the alpha male die, one of these males-in-waiting may take his place.

In African wild dogs, the alpha male dog assists the female while she is giving birth by licking away the amniotic membranes that surround the pups so they can take their first breath. During their early development he also helps by providing the pups with meat, guarding them and playing with them. The latter has an important role in teaching the pups about social relations, a matter of life and death in the dog clan. A dog rejected by its clan has little chance of surviving unless it is able to join a new clan. When alone its ability to hunt successfully is lowered and it becomes easy prey to other carnivorous species. Added to this, it is extremely stressful for a social species to be alone and the dog's physiological system changes so that it becomes more vulnerable to disease and other stress-related illnesses.

SEVEN

A pack of African wild dogs
setting off to hunt.

Hunting

Wild dogs are generally classified as hunters and, while it is true that they can all hunt, quite a number of canid species are omnivorous (both meat and plant eaters). They have a wide range of body weights (from 5 to 80 kilograms) and their dietary habits range from scavenging and omnivorous feeding to being strictly carnivorous. Some wild species eat fruit and berries and even vegetable matter. The dainty crab-eating zorros weigh only about 5 kilograms and they are omnivorous, consuming mostly fruit but also insects and land crabs. Eggs are also part of the diet of many canids, and crab-eating zorros often add turtle eggs to their diet.

Many of the canid species classified as carnivores (meat eaters) thrive on very small prey. For instance, the Ethiopian wolf is a solitary feeder and a rodent specialist. The solitary Arctic fox is similar, offering an odd sight to distant observers because it can be seen continually jumping into the air, turning in mid-air and literally diving head first straight into the snow, hind legs and tail wriggling. One can see this fox darting and pouncing for hours as it goes after rodents hidden under loose snow cover. Jackals are perhaps the best all-round feeders. They eat anything from eggs to lizards, from carrion to fruit, insects, frogs and even fish. Coyotes, often hunting alone, may form an intriguing hunting partnership with badgers. The strange pair works on the principle of a division of labour. The coyote's job is to locate the prey (the coyote's sense of smell is far superior to that of the badger) and the badger's job is then to make the prey available (the badger has powerful front paws that can dig up even very hard soil). This partnership works well for hunting rabbits and rodents that hide in deep burrows and under-ground chambers. While the badger digs, the coyote stands guard and catches the emerging rabbit or fleeing rodent. Both hunters then share the kill. Australian dingoes often hunt alone and they tend to specialise in rabbits and especially rabbit kittens. Since introduced rabbits can occur in plague proportions in Australia, these feeding activities of the dingoes can be beneficial for the ecology. Many species of wild canids prefer to be day feeders (diurnal) or twilight feeders (crepuscular) but most foxes and jackals have shifted almost exclusively to foraging at night (nocturnal), apparently because of the presence of humans. Despite popular perception none of these feeding habits evokes the image, or fits the reality, of a dangerous, stalking, lone hunter lying in ambush with an eye on living prey.

Indeed, when canids are dangerous and stalking large live prey, they are never alone. There is an inverse relationship in dogs between group size and food source. The more omnivorous a dog is, and the more readily it feeds on small prey (such as rodents), the more likely it will forage alone or in small groups. On the other hand, packs are a sign that they are likely to hunt for larger prey and stable packs suggest that large live prey is their dominant or only food source. In the world of carnivores this is very unusual. Only about 10 to 15 per cent of carnivores live in groups, and this includes wild dogs.

Groups of animals are normally subdivided into four different functional types: breeding, population (sharing the same home range), feeding (utilising the same food source together), and foraging (banding together while searching for food). The first group is the most common among all carnivores and the latter the least common. Breeding may be one of the factors requiring group formation for, at least, a short period. Group life in canids, however, is not just determined by the way they raise their young but also by the way they forage. If they want to access prey as strong or as large, or even larger, than themselves, they are bound for teamwork. For example, South American bush dogs often hunt in pairs or small packs and in this cooperative hunting effort they can bring down the capybara, a rodent as large as they are themselves.

The size of the pack varies with food types, topography, prey density, and overall population size of the species in a given region. There are also very important seasonal differences. That is, hunting parties may form only while the young are being reared, and only at those times are larger prey sought after. Once the young have dispersed, the pair might also disperse and hunt singly or occasionally in pairs for the rest of the season.

Hence, group stability and group size is partly determined by the need or preference to hunt specific kinds of prey or by the general availability of specific prey classes (ungulates versus rodents). In order to kill anything as large or larger than themselves, canids require a team effort.

Killing large prey

Most canids, such as African wild dogs, dholes and wolves, seeking larger live prey have tremendous stamina and can run and walk long distances in a day without ill effect. Grey wolves, in particular, are excellent runners and can stay with their prey for chases as long as 20 kilometres, reaching speeds up to 70 kilometres per hour. Although they do not have good vision for seeing shapes, they are able to see movement well, and they use this, as well as their ability to hear and their superior sense of smell, to locate and follow prey. Their extensive vocal repertoire may serve them well in hunting since it is a means of coordinating the hunt.

Despite their superior running skills, wild canids are not among the most efficient hunters. They cannot bring down large prey efficiently and quickly. They cannot even kill a rodent by biting alone but need to shake it vigorously to break its neck. Most canids have rather short canine teeth and curved upper incisors that serve as a pair of secondary incisors. Such dental construction cannot deliver a killing bite but is extremely good for holding of prey. The jaws of Indian dholes, in particular, also open wide enough so that their mouth can hold objects of large sizes. Dholes hold the prey by the nose to bring it down, with the help of others, and then disembowel their victim, by which time the victim has usually died of shock.

The one major objection and human disaffection to wild dogs who hunt large prey almost always relates to their method of killing. The beginning of a hunt to the victim's eventual death may take hours. It is messy, causes suffering and is difficult to watch without wanting to rescue the victim or at least wishing it a more speedy death. Large cats, by contrast, can crush the spine, sever the throat, strangle and suffocate a victim often in under a minute, sometimes in seconds. Coyotes and dingoes form an in-between group of hunters because both species are adapted to hunt small species when on their own, and large prey when their normal food supply is temporarily unavailable. In Australia, this is often necessary for dingoes in regions that suffer prolonged drought (over many years), leading to dwindling food supplies.

Dingoes are known to use deception during hunting and, in this respect, they are probably unique amongst canids. Unlike the 'honest' symbiosis between coyote and badger, dingoes may practise well-planned piracy even when hunting singly. In the tropical north of Australia, where magpie geese occupy the wetlands in their thousands, dingoes may stalk magpie geese in very demonstrative ways. As the magpie geese focus their attention on the dingo, a sea eagle or a swamp harrier swoops down from above and kills a distracted magpie goose. Magpie geese are too heavy for eagles or harriers to lift to a safe location so they have to devour them on site. It is then that the dingo rushes forward, chasing away the eagle or harrier and claiming a meal that, so it seems, has been killed solely for the dingo.

Very extensive studies have shown that dingoes may feed on 177 different prey species. However, only ten of these species constitute 80 per cent of the dingo's diet. The main fare includes larger prey. In order of preference they eat the red kangaroo, rabbit, swamp wallaby, cattle (carrion), dusky rat, magpie goose, brush-tail possum, long-haired rat, agile wallaby and common wombat. Having said this, there is a strange habit of some dingo populations to focus on one type of prey only and when that prey declines in number they will then not look for alternative sources and may eventually even die of starvation. However, others will even resort to eating grasshoppers (locusts) when normal prey has disappeared because of drought.

There is clear evidence that the dingo's success in hunting large kangaroos is higher when dingoes combine forces and operate in groups of three or more. For instance, a lone dingo may need twenty attempts to bail up and kill a red kangaroo while a hunting party of at least three succeeds on about every fifth attempt.

Among wolves, African wild dogs and dholes, in particular, the prey is 'tested' for its speed, alertness and fitness. In grey wolves, only 8 per cent of chases of large prey (such as moose) are successful. The 92 per cent that get away have either shown confidence and have continued running, thus merging back into the group, or they have employed their substantial armour of defences: hooves in moose and deer, or horns in bison. The young, sick, old or neglected are the ones that are usually taken by wild dogs. But even so, the process of gaining a catch is lengthy. Prey, perhaps four times the size of the wild dog, needs to be brought down through the constant simultaneous infliction of pain. Even then the victim is not killed outright but dies eventually from the sum total of its injuries or, mercifully, as in the case of sambars brought down by dholes, from the shock of being disembowelled.

The dhole is the only species of canid that employs extensive vocalisation as part of its hunting strategy. Unlike the open savannahs of Africa where prey and predator can often see each other, dholes may need to hunt in thick bush scrub. Their even fawn to light-brown coloured coats merge with that of the scrub so it is very easy for them to lose sight of each other. Vocal communication, therefore, replaces vision as a way of remaining in contact. Camouflage of potential prey may require one dog to alert all others when the prey has been spotted. Ambush is not entirely workable (especially since dholes can be so very noisy) but a technique of encircling works well in their bushy environment. While encircling the prey in dense underbrush, they use special repetitive whistle-like, high-pitched honks. It is not known whether the whistles have an intimidating effect on the prey but it is possible that whistling heard from all directions may make the victim stand still rather than run. Whistle vocalisations are also used when they reassemble their pack after a chase. Because of their unique and distinct calls, dholes have rightfully been named 'whistling hunters'. Bush dogs also vocalise while hunting but not as extensively as dholes.

Dholes also draw on many different items of prey, such as hares, chitals, sambars, field rats and wild pigs. Most kills are made in the early morning hours but occasionally also at other times during the day. They also eat a fruit called zizyphus that is favoured equally by humans, primates and bears. Of all prey species, there appears to be a preference for sambars, very large ungulates of about four times the size of dholes. For this quarry, the dholes have devised the very special technique of attacking in water, an environment where the strong sambar cannot utilise its hooves as a weapon. Dholes will also avoid making a kill close to their den. This is possibly so because in both national parks where dholes are protected (the Bandipur and Nagarole areas in Southern

India) tigers and leopards share the same terrain and would no doubt be drawn to a kill and thus endanger the den, if it were too near.

Amongst the predators of large prey, the red wolf is perhaps the most methodical. Generally needing a very large home range, the pack will hunt for seven to ten days in one area and then move to a different area, taking muskrats, rodents, rabbits, deer, hogs and carrion. Grey wolves, by contrast, find their prey by chance encounter. When olfactory or visual contact is established, they follow the prey. They may range nearly as far as 400 kilometres in a season. Their quarry is seasonally dependent and related to migratory habits of the prey species. They will hunt for deer (including the wapiti, a North American species), moose, caribou, bison, muskrats, mountain sheep and beavers, depending on availability. Notably, almost all types of prey are larger than themselves and, of all the canid hunters, grey wolves have the most stable clans.

Impact of group hunting

Wild dogs have no adverse effect on the population of their prey species, unless humans have hunted certain of their prey species to near extinction. Indeed, the co-evolution of prey and predators has ensured that they can coexist. It is not in the interest of predators to eliminate their food source, nor is it in the interest of the prey species to lose their healthiest reproducing adults.

Prey species have evolved some mechanisms whereby their interests are also maintained. One strategy for survival, particularly of grazing animals, is to travel in large herds. Generally speaking, the larger the herd, the smaller the impact of predators. This is true especially when territorial ranges bind predators while the herds are migratory. Second, most prey animals (such as ungulates) synchronise their time of giving birth to within a few days of each other. Although all ungulate newborns can rise to their feet and run within a few hours of birth, they are vulnerable and remain the most likely target of all predators, not just canids. By creating a sudden abundance of food, the saturation of the needs of predators ensures that many of the offspring survive. Indeed, the percentage of survival of newborn ungulates is higher than that of the offspring of predators, in each season and over a lifetime. A further strategy, employed by bovine species such as bison or buffalo, is to use cooperative defence strategies. For instance, they will form a protective cordon around the young to ensure the survival of more offspring.

Gazelles and other dainty ungulates, such as impala, are not strong enough for cooperative defences, yet even they have developed a range of strategies. One is a warning system via the tail. When they are running, it flashes and invites others to run in the same direction. It is usually only the one not following these signals that is caught. More importantly, every year, these ungulates produce a substantial surplus of males. In the diet of African wild dogs young male gazelles and wildebeest are the prey items most often chosen. That preference is related to the fact that they are easier to catch and therefore taken even if they have less meat. Herds of gazelles or wildebeest seem to offer up these young males to predators by the way they organise their social groups. Young gazelle males tend to form small clusters and are more often than not found on the very periphery of the group or herd. These behaviours alone predispose them to be selected by stalking predators. Moreover, young males tend to delay fleeing when the herd takes off and so, by being at the tail end of the fleeing group, they are more easily caught.

Advantages of group hunting

For hunters of prey, as are most wild dogs, there are clear advantages of being in groups and most have to do with successfully obtaining and maintaining food. Dogs are not as efficient hunters as are large cats. A single lion can bring down a sizeable prey by itself, not so much because of its strength but because of the construction of its teeth. The teeth can deliver a killing bite very swiftly. A single lion is therefore able to seek out the same range of prey that it would choose if hunting in a pride. Wild dog species, however, can only succeed in taking down prey as large as, or larger than, they are themselves if they make a team effort. Having more eyes to see and more scent detectors, they are also more likely to locate a food source. Then there is the speed with which a kill can be made. The time line here is clear: one dog requires much longer (and more energy) hunting larger prey (of rabbit size and larger) than do pairs or packs. Furthermore, the chasing distance decreases. It has been shown for African wild dogs that an increase in the number of dogs per pack decreases the distance of the chase. So they can catch their prey sooner and, therefore, with less expenditure of energy. Some dingoes near wetlands and lakes often use a special technique to flush out swans. One dingo approaches stealthily and openly forces the swans to retreat. They usually do so not knowing that there is a second dingo hiding in the direction of their retreat. Then the dingo begins to run and in that moment of confusion, the second dingo strikes. In many of these cases, it would be impossible for an individual to catch a flighted bird, such as the swan, on its own.

As well as the reduced speed of achieving a kill successfully, there is also the reduced number of attempts made by the hunter. To run and hunt twenty times before a successful kill is made, as compared to running only five times, means that the energy expenditure is four times as large for an individual and may be in inverse proportion to its dietary needs. The individual may go hungry for days and, if very hungry, may also not continue to have the sustained energy to make the next attempt successful. In other words, a ratio of one success for twenty attempts is not viable for survival, while one for five attempts is.

Another clear advantage of group hunting is that, in dogs as compared to large cats, it broadens the range of prey species available to the pack. Instead of having to rely on a few prey species of limited protein value and weight, the group faces a much wider choice of species by being able to include in their target prey group a variety of species that are larger and would be unobtainable even in pair-hunting teams. Increased choice also increases availability and increased availability, in turn, should lead to larger amounts of food being consumed.

Finally, and very importantly, a group of dogs is more likely to keep the kill while it is being eaten than is a dog alone with its kill. In the plains of Africa and even in some regions of Asia, any kill is at once heavily contested. This is referred to as interspecies competition. Hyenas in Africa and feline species, vultures, crows and many others may steal the kill almost the moment that it has been made unless the canid predators have the numbers to keep the hungry competitors at bay, at least long enough for one full feed to be obtained by each member of the hunting group. This might be a good reason to ensure that the ratio of dogs to hyenas is very high, so that the dogs can assert their rights over a kill.

Levels of intraspecies competition—the competition amongst themselves at a food site—may also determine interspecies competition. There are some canid groups in which competition at the food site is low and others in which it is very high. For instance, in dholes, competition at food sites is almost entirely absent and it has been rightly asked by researchers whether this lack of competition might be due to food abundance. Ecological factors could certainly play a role. Dholes hunt in dense habitat and have small home ranges because their prey is rather sedentary and available at higher density throughout the year than is the case for wolves or even African wild dogs. High food competition, as observed in dingoes or wolves, may be related to food scarcity. However, in our opinion, it may be crucially related to other factors, because food competition is almost the same at times of food abundance as it is at times of scarcity. One factor may be the degree to which a kill is contested by other members of the same species (intraspecies competition) and this may be related to vertical hierarchy within the group, imposing a strict feeding order and resulting in conflict when one individual transgresses.

Some studies have found that group-hunting canids may have a six- to twelve-fold higher food intake when hunting in groups so that the net benefits actually increase with an increase in pack size. Benefits derived from group hunting obviously function within a certain minimum and optimal range. When the pack (not the clan) gets too large and they still only bring down the same number and kind of prey, eventually the food intake per individual drops, but for a group of seven a kill of a larger prey offers plenty of food for all and even enables other smaller groups from the clan to join and clear the carcass completely.

Disadvantages of group hunting

Groups are usually not as mobile and they are more visible than a single individual. This means they can be detected more easily by predators. Hunters living in groups may often get less food than solitary hunters, because there are more mouths to feed and, although group hunting is more successful, the number of successful hunting attempts may not always match the increased food needs of the group if the group gets beyond a certain threshold size and becomes very large. Compared to hunting in pairs or alone, hunting in groups is more complicated because of the need to coordinate the activities of all members. These disadvantages of group hunting seem to be at the forefront of why some species of canids are endangered (wolves and dholes in particular) while others that are more asocial, such as foxes and coyotes, are able to thrive even under very adverse human influence.

Of course, hunting in groups could be solely for hunting, a convenient strategy of foraging together. It may not necessarily require that the hunting-group members breed together or commonly share the same territory. Yet hunting strategy, while fostering a certain level of social life together, cannot by itself account for the different group sizes in which canids live. In fact, no single factor can explain group size, because it depends on many factors, including competition between canids and other species, strictness or openness of group territoriality and prey preferences.

Hunting, intelligence and aggression

Another important point in relation to hunting in co-ordinated groups is that hunters do not simply run along with each other. Hunting is a well-coordinated intentional activity, as shown by the examples of the encircling techniques and whistling calls of the dholes, the 'testing' techniques used by wolves, and the ambush of swans by dingoes. It is not clear whether group hunting is always entirely driven by hunger and necessity: there may be circumstances when hunting is intentional and planned. Wild dogs have the choice to hunt alone, in pairs or in groups. They make different choices at different times. A number of hunters who are sometimes or mostly solitary hunters (such as the maned wolf, coyotes, most foxes and jackals) will hunt with their partner or even also with their offspring for a season. So most canids find themselves hunting alone and in small or large groups at some time in their life. Recent studies of coyotes have found that hunger is motivationally unrelated to hunting in inexperienced coyotes and that the relationship between hunger, killing and feeding is complex and not nearly as well understood as we once thought.

We do know, however, that planned activities, such as hunts, have at times been regarded as evidence of intelligence. For example, the hunting group expeditions carried out by chimpanzees to kill and then eat a favourite monkey species (colobine monkeys) have been hailed as being a clear sign of higher cognition unique among animals. The argument that cooperative hunting is evidence of 'intelligence' in chimpanzees is largely based on the assumption that, in their case, hunting is seen as a deliberate, planned and coordinated act. Are wild dogs so different? Most pack hunting dogs would fulfil the same characteristics of intelligence because they too have alternative foraging activities available to them. In order to capture food several times their own size and strength, their techniques need to be very well coordinated indeed. Chimpanzees are certainly not unique, either in performing the activity of hunting or in the degree to which they coordinate their activity with other group members, but the tendency has been to attribute different functions to similar behaviours, calling hunting 'intelligent' in one species and 'motivational' in another (the dog).

The argument in defence of this differentiation is that chimpanzees do not need to hunt for their food by killing, whereas carnivores, such as many wild dogs, are seen to be driven by that need. It may well be true that chimpanzees may not be driven by hunger to hunt and kill because they have other sources of food. Their acts of killing thus do not seem derived from necessity but from a kind of wilful malice. However, not all foods are consumed for reasons of hunger. Some animals ingest stones to aid digestion, some parrots fly long distances to feed on stony outcrops in order to obtain important minerals.

Chimpanzees may require occasional high doses of protein and their acts may follow some specific physiological cravings rather more similar to the parrots seeking minerals than to malice or hunger. Meat provides proteins in an efficient and concentrated form and it is possible that its ingredients are at times essential or desirable additives for the chimpanzee diet.

If one can argue that hunting indicates higher intelligence in primates, as many do, dogs therefore also show 'intelligence'. Indeed, humans have trained many breeds of dogs to perform a series of complicated tasks, be this in the army, in drug detection, crime control, in providing sight or ears for sight- or hearing-impaired people and in tracking skiers lost in mountains. In all these various roles some individual dogs have shown amazing aptitude, discipline and insight.

Hunting is not in itself an 'aggressive' act in the sense that killing occurs as a result of emotions. There is no 'anger' against the victim, there is no 'hatred', there are no foolish acts of running out just for the sake of hurting another. Sometimes neighbouring groups may kill each other in acts of aggression but this is usually over *territorial* claims, not directly about *hunting*. Indeed, if emotions did play a role in hunting, the cautious timing, observation and sheer concentration required to successfully capture a most reluctant living participant may be impaired and the ability to succeed would be greatly diminished. In fact, studies have found no correlation between aggression and killing success.

If we want to look for aggression, we need to look into the social life of group-living animals. It appears that aggression of canids, be this at feeding sites, in daily life, around dens or among rivals, is related to group complexity and, specifically, to vertical hierarchies. Such hierarchies exist equally amongst chimpanzees and gorillas, as well as in stable packs of wild dogs.

Hierarchy, group complexity and feeding

Being an alpha male or alpha female in a canid clan (holding the highest status) is a matter of power and of breeding rights. It is not correlated to killing success. The top dog does not need to be the best hunter in order to be the top dog. Competition in canid societies, if any, comes from within the ranks as a social issue and is not related to performance criteria such as providing the most food. Criteria, such as appearing and looking confident, and the adherence to social rituals by subordinates, all fall into the precincts of power.

Vertical hierarchies in stable groups may give more cohesion and stability because life is organised and regulated by a series of ritualised and stereotyped acts. But at the same time, opportunity also exists to break the rules. A vertical hierarchy invites harmony at one level but when conflict occurs it can lead to serious outcomes. Vertical hierarchies can, at times, also be semitransparent and allow for a small trickle of 'upward mobility'. That is, the top dog may not always remain the top dog.

In wolf society, a group of young males may turn on an alpha male and expel or even kill him.

The effects of a complex hierarchy can be seen by observing the behaviour of a hungry group at the site of a favourite food source. In wolf society, the alpha male and female will feed first and their subordinates usually have to wait until they have had their fill, although they tend to try at their own risk. These rules are generally non-negotiable. By contrast, in groups of African wild dogs, all dogs will feed together and at the same time without much jostling and little, if any, competition. This is also true of a number of other canid species, such as dholes or bush dogs.

Such very different social rules in different species of canids may have developed or evolved because of environmental conditions. For instance, African wild dogs live in a very predator-rich environment. They are surrounded by species larger than themselves (or more numerous) who feed on the same foods as they do. The contestation for a kill is enormous: lions, leopards and other cats, hyenas, jackals, vultures and even crocodiles (if near water) are powerful contenders and they will steal the fresh kill when given half a chance, as we said before. African wild dogs do not have time to waste on rituals reasserting who will be the first to feed. They would never be able to feed the pack and the kill would be gone before even the first had a chance to get their fill. Engrossed in their own affairs, they could even be killed themselves because they are less vigilant when they are focused on feeding.

Wolves, however, have functioned in environments in Europe, Asia and in North America where predator contestation is far lower than on the African plains. Bears are nearly omnivorous and do not depend entirely on meat to survive. In winter months when food is scarce, they are in hibernation and therefore not competing for a kill, and in summer they usually find sufficient other foods, such as berries and fish. Cats, including tigers, are solitary hunters and smaller cats are unable to compete against a pack of wolves. A tiger might contest a kill but a tiger's territory is so large that a meeting can usually be avoided. In short, the contestation from other predators is minimal so they can afford to maintain a system of contestation and competition among groups of their own species.

Complexity of social systems thus depends partly on the enemies of that species. Chimpanzees, gorillas and wolves do not have many enemies (other than humans!) and their social systems reflect this. Species who are more vulnerable to predation have a different kind of social system: the level of cooperation they need for survival leaves less time for infighting and conflict within the group. The wolf's complex social system and the expressiveness of the individual, as well as its superior communication skills, make it the ideal companion of humans. Both species have evolved similarly complex and hierarchical social systems. All domestic dogs were derived from the grey wolf (see Chapter 1) and we can easily see why such an unusual cross-species friendship would have become so very widespread and so durable over more than one hundred thousand years.

EIGHT

The red fox's craftiness is
actually a sign of its intelligence.

Intelligent behaviour

Intelligent behaviour is often understood to include the ability to learn and remember, adapt and be flexible according to circumstances, solve problems, use complex communication, follow the attention of others, and to be able to direct the attention of other members of the social group to particular locations, and to use tools. It can also refer to the ability to predict the behaviour of others and so be able to deceive them, and to empathise with the feelings and needs of others. In the Canidae family, the mix all of these different patterns of behaviour is so varied and so difficult to determine that it makes little sense to say that one species of canid is more or less intelligent than another. We can say that each species has particular adaptations that ensure its survival and that some species might be more flexible in changing their behaviour to meet new demands than are others, but it is invalid to rank canid species in any order of intelligence.

Owners of domestic dogs are often keen to know whether they have an intelligent dog or whether a particular breed is more or less intelligent than another. In response to this, Stanley Coren has developed a 'canine IQ test', composed of simple problems that the dog has to solve or to learn and remember. While it might be interesting to test dogs in this way, the final score achieved by any dog has little meaning as some sort of accurate score of 'intelligence', either for one individual dog versus another, or one breed versus another. How a dog performs any task is dependent on its past experience, its relationship to its owner (or whoever is testing the dog), its emotional state and its motivation to eat the small food rewards offered in some of the tests. Breeds of domestic dogs may differ in their performance on the different kinds of tests, some being better at solving particular problems and others at learning and remembering certain things, but the IQ test does not reveal to us some unitary characteristic that we can call intelligence. It might be more accurate to say that dogs have many different kinds of 'intelligences'.

What do we know of the intelligences of the different species of canids? There have been few attempts to test the performance of wild dogs on standard tests and, of course, the canine IQ test would be inappropriate since it depends on interaction between a dog and its owner. But, to attempt to answer the question, we can discuss what complex behaviour patterns have been observed in wild dogs. For the most part we have to rely on anecdotal evidence collected by researchers who have observed canids in the wild or, in a few cases, in captivity. A number of experiments that have been carried out on domestic dogs also provide information about the capacity of the family Canidae.

Ability to learn and remember

There is no doubt that canids can learn and that they have extremely detailed and long memories. Numerous accounts of the memories of domestic dogs for their owners or familiar locations testify to this. Many reports tell also of wolves that have remembered individuals over very long periods of time.

Wolves are also known for their masterful ability to learn by observation. People in the United States who have kept grey wolves in captivity note, time and time again, that they learn to open latches and gates by observing what their keepers do. One observation of the gate latch being opened seems to be sufficient for them to learn. Domestic dogs do not learn this under similar circumstances. Added to this, wolves will wait until the coast is clear before they make an escape. That takes planning ahead, which is another aspect of intelligence. They have also been noted to open the doors of other cages containing wolves before making their escape. Perhaps this assistance of the other is typical 'clan' behaviour.

In contrast to their ability to learn to escape, wolves kept in human company are not willing to learn tricks or other human-designed tasks for food rewards. In other words, they cannot be conditioned in the same way as can domestic dogs. They do not conform to human demands, such as following at heal on a leash or sitting on command. Seemingly this is because they have not shared 100 000 years of living mutually with humans, as have domestic dogs, and so are not motivated to learn the tasks that we might want to teach them. Wolves, and presumably other wild canids, do not have the 'obedience' that we find in domestic dogs. Some people describe domestic dogs as being just smart enough to learn what we want to teach them and just dumb enough to do it, but really the difference between wild and domestic canids may have more to do with temperament and emotional responses to humans rather than anything to do with intelligence. Wild canids are likely to be very willing to learn from each other. In fact, such social learning is essential for cooperation between members of a clan or even within the type of family group that is typical of foxes.

Ability to adapt and be flexible

We often speak of intelligence in terms of flexibility and creativity. To this we can add the ability to adapt to different circumstances and conditions, whether this is applied to individuals or to the species as a whole. The conditions to which the animal, or species, must adapt may be physical (changes in temperature or availability of food) or behavioural (changed social circumstances). The ability of wild dogs to survive in differing climatic conditions depends on adapting their behaviour to meet the specific demands of the different environments, and the canids seem to be particularly able to do this successfully. For example, since its introduction to Australia only 160 years ago, the red fox has broadened its range from the relatively benign regions of south-eastern Australia to the harsh climates of the desert and the cold Snowy Mountains. To survive in these different conditions the foxes have to adopt different patterns of using their dens, accept different foods and, presumably, use different hunting strategies. Some might say that this reflects a kind of 'species intelligence' but, in our opinion, this is stretching the meaning of 'intelligence' too far.

Perhaps one of the most obvious examples of adaptation made in the family Canidae was that of grey wolves about 100 000 years ago when they started living close to humans and scavenging on our food scraps and other wastes. This was apparently the first step towards domestication and the evolution of all domestic dogs. But only some of the grey wolves made this change in their lifestyle. Where they the more or less intelligent members of their species? They certainly showed adaptability and flexibility. Of course, the process of living in closer contact with humans is unlikely to have occurred as a single step within one generation of wolves but gradually over a number of generations. Therefore, it is not likely to be an example of some kind of individual adaptation, although individual dogs vary considerably in their flexibility and ability to adapt.

Past experience has a strong influence on the adaptability of dogs. Stressful events in early life can alter an individual's responses to novel situations profoundly, as we know from a number of species. Even stress before birth, which is transmitted to the developing foetus from the mother, has marked effects on an individual's behaviour. The stressed offspring are more fearful of new situations than unstressed ones, and this fear can interfere with their ability to learn. They also explore and play less than unstressed members of the same species and show impaired ability to cope with stressful situations. Hence, the net affect of this prenatal stress is reduced flexibility of the individual. We may interpret this as a lowering of intelligence, but we believe that these results illustrate that there is no fixed or unitary aspect of an individual that can be described by the term intelligence, or at least it shows that so-called intelligent behaviour can be radically modified by early experience and even experience before birth.

Individuals that have experienced stress prenatally show not only changed behaviour but also changes in the secretion of certain hormones. In particular, they have abnormally high levels of the stress hormone, cortisol, circulating in the blood. This can have long-term effects on their immune system and susceptibility to stress-related diseases.

An experimental study examined the effects of prenatal stress on Arctic foxes. The foxes studied were in captivity and stress was applied prenatally by the experimenter taking some of the pregnant females from their cages and holding them for one minute per day once a day during the last third of their pregnancies. Other mothers were not stressed in this way. The hormone levels of all of the offspring were measured when the offspring, called kits, were ten days old. Those born to stressed mothers were found to have higher levels of cortisol, and also of another hormone, pro-gesterone, than the kits of unstressed mothers. Both of these hormones are associated with particular patterns of behaviour, and the elevated levels of cortisol indicate that the prenatally stressed kits were more fearful and at greater risk of disease than kits not stressed prena-tally. Hence, the stress of close contact with a human affected the next generation. Other studies have shown that it may even affect the second and third generations to follow.

Quite apart from the issue of intelligence, this study is very important in showing us the marked effects of taking a wild canid and breeding it in captivity. Human contact is much more stressful than we would expect, even when it is well meaning.

Finally, on the topic of flexibility, recent research has shown that dogs are extremely flexible in the way that they process spatial information (the whereabouts of things). They can readily switch between different cues that provide them with spatial information. Experiments were conducted using one set of those cues that involved spatial coordinates with respect to the dogs themselves (called egocentric cues) and another set that involved the spatial relationships between objects in the surrounding world (called allocentric cues). The dogs used these two quite different sets of information with ease and it is likely that this ability is essential to effective hunting. When hunting, the dog needs to take into account its own position relative to other members of its pack, the location of the prey and the locations of obstacles in the way.

Ability to solve problems

Canids have to solve problems related to both their physical environment and social organisation, such as how to find food, negotiate barriers in the landscape, and function effectively in social situations. Very few systematic reports of such problem solving in the wild have been reported, so we must rely on reports of problem solving by canids in captivity or of domestic dogs tested in controlled experimental conditions.

The main problem faced by wild dogs kept in captivity is how to escape. We have mentioned above that wolves are quick to learn how to escape but, failing the opportunity of opening the gate latch to escape, the captive wolf has no alternative other than going over the fence. Some do just this by climbing even several metres of fencing wire. In their book *Dogs: A Startling New Understanding of Canine Origin, Behavior, and Evolution*, Raymond and Lorna Coppinger report the difficulty of keeping coyotes in captivity. They were conducting an experiment in which they were raising coyote pups and border collie pups at the same time. One day they saw a coyote climb the wire-mesh fence and walk along the top rail to reach the cage containing the collies. This alerted the Coppingers to the possibility that the coyotes were getting in and out of the cage at will. To test this they sprinkled flour on the ground outside the cages before they left for the night. Next morning they saw numerous coyote footprints in the flour and deduced that each night the coyotes escaped from their cages to hunt mice in the field and returned to be with the collies during the day. The collies apparently did not follow suit but similar behaviour has been observed on occasion in domestic dogs.

One of the authors (Lesley) had an English wire-haired terrier, which she left at home when she went to work. He was a distinctive, large and shaggy dog, called Sam, and there had been reports that Sam had been seen crossing the main road at the lights and making his way through the shopping area. These were dismissed as being cases of mistaken identity until one day Sam was missing when she came home from work earlier than usual. Just half an hour before the time when she usually returned home Sam jumped over the back fence to take up his usual 'waiting' position at the back door. From then on Sam was observed to repeat this pattern several times, until his escape route was blocked.

Over many years, researchers have used 'detour tasks' to assess the intelligence or, as it is more commonly called now, 'cognitive ability' of different species. These tasks involve placing a barrier between the animal being tested and something it is motivated to reach, such as its food bowl or some companions. The time taken by the test animal to figure out that it has to turn and go around the barrier to reach its goal is seen as an indication of its intelligence. Although amongst species there are interesting differences in performance on detour tasks, it is doubtful that they represent any meaningful comparison of intelligence. Whereas one species might prefer to go around barriers because that is a strategy for survival, another species might prefer to push through barriers as an equally effective strategy in its own environment. As an example of the latter, animals living in tall grass would be familiar with pushing through visual barriers and, in the experimental situation, might try this strategy first before deciding to go around the barrier. An additional problem with comparisons between species, and also between individuals of the same species, is how to be sure that the animals being tested are equally motivated to reach the goal. For these reasons, detour tests are not reliable for making comparisons about intelligence but they can

provide some interesting information about how individual animals perform and whether they can learn by
observing how others solve the detour problem. In
fact, it has been shown that domestic dogs learn to go
around a V-shaped barrier by watching a human
carrying out the detour problem. Interestingly, the dog
watches the human and learns to go around the barrier
but does not follow the exact path taken by the human.
Once the dog realises that the problem can be solved it
interpolates the solution to follow its own preferred
path. This is thought to be an example of 'social
learning' and we might well consider that it occurs from
one dog to another (each dog learns by watching
another dog perform the task). Wild canids are likely
to make good use of social learning to pass information
from one individual to the next. In most species, the
main route for passing acquired patterns of behaviour
on from one generation to the next is from mother to
offspring, but in group-living canids there would be
ample opportunity for learned patterns of behaviour
to be passed from any older members of the clan to
younger ones.

Use of complex communication

The complexity of the communication signals used by
canids suggests that they communicate about many things
and that they might do so intentionally. If the animal has
no control over making the signals, they may merely be

an expression of its emotional state. But if they are intentional, signals may have referential meaning (refer to an object or another animal) and be used like a rudimentary language to communicate about external objects or other animals. A series of experiments has shown that both vervet monkeys and domestic chickens use referential signals to warn other members of their species about the presence of specific predators. Vervet monkeys use different calls to signal the presence of a leopard, snake or eagle, and the chicken uses a very different call for an aerial predator (such as an eagle) and predator on the ground (a raccoon). Other members of the signaller's species respond appropriately to the call: for example, the chicken crouches and remains stationary on hearing an alarm call for an aerial predator and struts with loud clucking on hearing the ground-predator alarm call, this being an attempt to drive the predator away.

It takes one further step to prove that the communication is intentional: the signaller should make the alarm calls only when another member of its species is present. This is known to be the case for the chicken at least: a rooster gives the aerial alarm call only when he is in the presence of one or more hens. This means that the signaller can control when he signals and only signals when there is a reason to do so.

So far the only research investigating whether canids use intentional and referential signalling has been carried out on domestic dogs communicating with humans, which is covered in the next section.

Understanding words

Domestic dogs respond appropriately to many different verbal commands given by humans. Are they aware of the meaning of the words or simply responding to the emotional content? It is often said that dogs have simply learned to associate certain words with certain actions and contexts and that they do not really know the meaning of the words. This claim is based on experiments in which dogs were given commands via an intercom rather than directly by a human that they could see. Dogs usually ignore these commands. The reason often given is that they need other non-verbal cues from the human and cannot respond to the words alone. But this explanation does not take into account the fact that dogs have superior hearing and, therefore, the command played to them by the intercom might sound so distorted to them (e.g. altered in frequency range) that they ignore it. Added to this, some domestic dogs respond appropriately to such an extensive range of words or simple phrases (over one hundred) that it seems unlikely that they are merely responding to the emotional content of the spoken words or to gestures that accompany them. This fact does not, of course, provide evidence that dogs respond to the meaning of spoken words but it does suggest that this is as a strong possibility. Whether or not dogs do or do not understand any aspects of human language is not known and will not be known until controlled experiments are conducted to find out. So far, such experiments have been carried out on chimpanzees and one species of parrot but not on dogs.

Following the attention of others

If one individual is looking at something, another individual might turn to look in the same direction in order to discover what is so interesting. This act almost certainly requires higher cognition because the second individual is likely to be aware that the first one is attending to something external to itself. In other words, the second individual has to be aware that the first one has its own separate interests and thoughts. Researchers interested in finding out whether animals are conscious look to see if they follow the direction of another's gaze.

Experiments have shown that domestic dogs will follow the direction of a human's gaze or that of another dog to locate food. In the case of dog–dog interactions of this kind they may also follow the direction in which the ears of the dog are focused. Dogs will even follow the direction in which a person glances without turning the head. This shows that the dog attends carefully to the person's eyes. It came as somewhat of a surprise when dogs were found to be better than chimpanzees at understanding eye-glancing signals made by humans. The difference between dogs and chimpanzees could result from the stronger bonds formed between domestic dogs and humans than between the chimpanzees and humans, at least under the laboratory conditions in which the chimpanzees were raised and tested. But this may not be the whole explanation for the difference between dogs and chimpanzees since some evidence suggests that, when chimpanzees make a choice between two objects, they do not take any notice of looking or pointing clues given by another chimpanzee.

Dogs do attend carefully to other dogs' eyes and use them to communicate. Glancing may also be used by dogs to communicate with humans: domestic dogs often communicate that they want food by glancing back and forth from the food bowl to their owner.

These experiments on domestic dogs show that communication by the eyes is important in referential signalling. We also know that the eyes convey many other important signals in dogs: in wolves a wide-eyed stare signals aggression and hence the likelihood of attack. All this evidence indicates strongly that wild canids may communicate with each other by eye glancing. They might well communicate by eye glancing during pack hunting or in the presence of an intruder to the pack. The cooperation involved in pack hunting requires a group decision about when to set off on a hunt, and communication about the location of the prey and which way to move in on it. Canids may use glances, as well as vocalisations, to signal the information needed to coordinate these activities.

Domestic dogs will also turn to look in the direction in which a human points. Pointing is often used by farmers to signal to their dogs when herding sheep and by human hunters using so-called gundogs to retrieve their kill. Dogs themselves cannot point with a hand but they do point with their heads and bodies, as seen in an extreme form in the 'pointer' breed. A less stylised form of head and body pointing has been seen in wolves and is likely used as a form of communication in many species of wild canids. One study that looked at the ability of two grey wolves, born and raised in a zoo, to follow the direction of pointing or gazing by humans to locate food hidden in a box, found that they were unable to do so. From this result, the researchers concluded that the ability to follow the direction of human pointing might be unique to domestic dogs, having evolved during their long period of mutual association. Although this interpretation of the result might be generally correct, the question remains whether the wolves failed to follow the signals given by humans because they were unable to do so or, simply, whether they chose not to do so because they had not bonded sufficiently with humans. It is quite possible that the wolves would have followed signals indicating the direction of the food source had they been given by another wolf. Also, of course, no one would be prepared to draw any general conclusions about what wolves can or cannot do from testing only two subjects in the most unnatural context of a zoo. We do know that one dog will follow pointing by another dog using the body as the pointer instead of the arm and hand as in the case of human pointing.

Predicting the behaviour of others

Hunting in a pack is one of the best examples of being able to predict the behaviour of others. Such tactics must be based on previous experience with the prey and from skills learned while growing up in the clan. A hunter that simply runs after its prey and uses superior speed to run it down need not make any complex tactical predictions. But canids that hunt large mammals plan the time to attack and use clever strategies to stalk and corner their prey before they simply run it down (see Chapter 7).

During the hunt each dog in the team must be aware of what the other dogs are doing and be able to predict their behaviour efficiently. In fact, the decision for the pack of dogs to set out together on a hunt seems to require each being aware of the intent of the others.

Predicting the behaviour of the prey may even involve deception. Coyotes have been seen hunting in pairs in which one bounds around and rolls in full view of the prey, to distract its attention, while the other remains in hiding until the prey is sufficiently off-guard for the attack to go unnoticed until it is too late.

Empathising

Owners of pet dogs usually say that their dog is able to empathise with their feelings because the dog becomes miserable when they are miserable and happy when they are happy and so on. But the dog may simply be mimicking its owner's behaviour rather than actually feeling what its owner feels. It is difficult to prove otherwise. However, if a dog carries out a specific action depending on the emotional state of its owner, we have some indication that it may be aware of how its owner feels or is thinking. Dogs can be trained to seek help when their owner is in trouble. For example, they can be trained to assist people with epilepsy by going to the telephone and pressing the appropriate button to obtain help when their owner is having a seizure. There is even some evidence that the dog can anticipate the onset of a seizure by a short interval. Of course, this is conditioned behaviour—the dogs are trained specifically for this task—but there are many cases in which even untrained dogs will seek help for their owners when problems arise and will lead a helper to their owner. We believe that there are too many such reports to dismiss them as mere coincidence but we also recognise that they do not prove that the dogs are able to empathise.

Using tools

Some species use tools to obtain food. A well-known example is the chimpanzees' use of a twig, which they insert into a termites' nest to fish out termites to eat. Chimpanzees also use tools to crack open nuts: a stone is used as a hammer to strike the nut placed on a tree root or anvil stone. A recent observation discovered tool manufacture as well as tool use in the crows of New Caledonia.

Using their beaks, the birds cut quite precisely shaped tools from pandanus leaves and use them to probe insects from holes in trees. No similar use of a tool has, as far as we know, been seen in wild canids. But this absence should not be taken as a comparative lack of intelligence in dogs since the environment in which the canids live and the food they eat may not demand the use of tools. As canids are equipped with powerful jaws and teeth, they would appear to have little need of tools to obtain food. Added to this the absence of hands would make tool using of the conventional kind less likely to occur in canids, the use of tools by the crows notwithstanding.

Another kind of tool using has been observed, although only in one subject. A captive coyote was seen to use food baits as tools to attract a chicken into his clutches. He saved some of his usual meal and placed several pieces near the fence of his cage. He then took hide as the chickens came pecking for the morsels of food. As one eventually took the piece of food closest to his hiding spot, he pounced and so obtained his preferred food in place of the food pieces that had become tools. This speaks strongly for the intelligence of canids, whatever we mean by that word, but more studies are needed to confirm these observations.

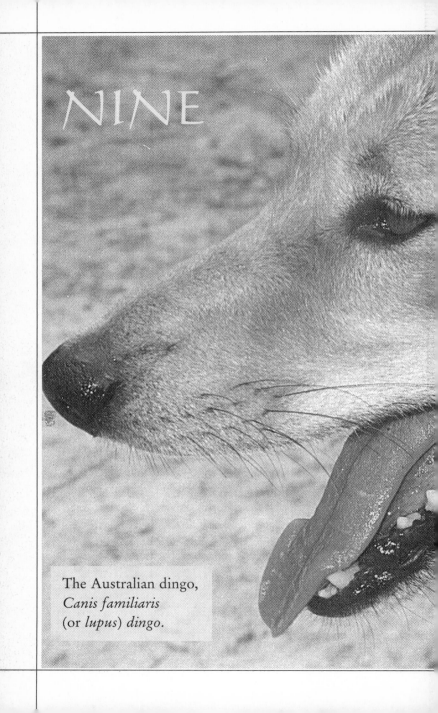

NINE

The Australian dingo,
Canis familiaris
(or *lupus*) *dingo*.

Domestic and feral dogs

Some researchers consider that the difference between wolves and domestic dogs, even those of today, is not great enough to place them in separate species. They prefer to separate them only at the level of subspecies, calling the domestic dog *Canis lupus familiaris* to indicate they share the species *lupus* with wolves. But this terminology is not officially accepted and domestic dogs are still referred to as a different species, *Canis familiaris*.

Over the thousands of years of close contact, dogs and humans might have influenced each other's evolution. Humans may have become increasingly reliant on the dog's sense of smell and to such an extent that the sensitivity of their own sense of smell diminished. There is no concrete evidence of this, apart from the fact that the structure of the human nasal cavity decreased in size. There is actually no way of comparing our ancestors' ability to smell with our own because sensory ability can only be measured in living organisms. Reduction in size of a sensory organ may indicate that use of this sensory organ has diminished but the size of a sensory organ is not the only characteristic determining its function.

David Paxton has hypothesised that humans lost some of their ability to smell as the shape of their face changed and became flatter, and it was this change in the shape of the face together with changes in the voice-producing apparatus that made speech possible. These changes, he suggests, were intimately linked to the bond between dogs and our human ancestors because the dogs took over the job of smelling, thus forming a dog–human unit with excellent olfaction as well as the ability to speak. Whether we owe our ability to speak to dogs is highly speculative although interesting. Many other changes in human lifestyle occurred at the same time as the human–dog bond was strengthening. Any or many of these could have been associated with the evolution of speech.

Nevertheless, dogs and humans must have altered each other's lives. As they adapted to living closely with each other, human culture changed and so did the social life of dogs.

In some ways, dogs related to humans as if they were other members of the clan but in other ways they adopted patterns of behaviour that were new and unique to the interspecies human–dog bond. In particular, domestic dogs acquired new ways of communicating, which were, apparently, easier for humans to understand. For example, most breeds of domestic dogs hold their tails up higher than wolves. Wolves do hold their tail up above horizontal when they adopt a threat posture but most domestic dogs in the same posture arch the tail over their backs. Other changes that took place with domestication were the earlier onset of sexual maturity and the loss of the seasonal breeding cycle characteristic of wolves.

Despite the long contact between wolves and humans, the appearance of these wolves (or dogs) did not begin to differ greatly from the grey wolf until about 12 000 to 14 000 years ago, when some human societies must have started to play an active role in breeding dogs with particular physical features or temperaments. This shift coincided with an important transition in the lifestyle of humans in some parts of the world, who shifted from being hunter–gathers to agriculturalists. Along with this change, humans may have found other ways to use dogs— for example, to guard their livestock and dwellings—which might have led them to breed different types of dogs.

The appearance of the dog's skull and other parts of its skeleton began to change under these pressures of selection by humans, and this is evident in archaeological records. The earliest of these have been found in the Middle East: one in a cave in Iraq and another in Israel in what was obviously a grave. These sites have been dated to about 13 000 years ago. In addition to these earliest sites, a large number of archaeological sites with

Canis familiaris bones have been dated to between 7000 and 9000 years ago. These have been found in many parts of the world, including Asia, Europe, North America and South America.

It is probable that humans in many different parts of the world began to breed different types of domestic dogs, depending on how they wanted to use them. Some dogs must have been selected to be good hunters, others good for guarding the farms or flocks and perhaps others for their affection and cute appearance. The discovery of a 5000 to 6000 year old site in China with three types of dogs of differing sizes and shapes shows that selective breeding of dogs may have occurred very early in that part of the world. From their paintings, frescos and writings, we know that the Romans might have developed some of the main breed-types familiar to us today. They used some breeds of dogs to guard their homes, as we do today, and others for military purposes. They had different types of dogs to work as messengers and others to attack during battles. The Greeks are known to have used guard dogs also, and this is likely to have been the source of their mythological three-headed dog, Cerberus, who guarded the gates of the underworld.

Once humans began to breed dogs, they continued and increased their efforts at different times in different places. A large number of current breeds of dogs originated within the last few hundred years and the first pedigrees of breeds were compiled in the nineteenth century, at a time when the first kennel clubs were formed.

Humans and the spread of dogs

Once wolves and humans had developed lifestyles of mutual dependence, they must have moved from one area to another together. This human-assisted dispersal of dogs has been an ongoing process. Some people think it possible that the now extinct Falkland Island wolf (*Dusicyon autralis*) descended from a domesticated dog taken to the island by humans. After that it became feral. This hypothesis is based on the fact that the remains of domestic dogs have been found in a cave in Southern Chile and dated to about 6000 to 8000 years ago, and also on some rather scanty evidence that the Falkland Island wolf was more similar in appearance to members of the genus *Canis* than to any members of the South American genus *Dusicyon*. It is also possible that the Falkland Island wolf's closest relative is the coyote and, therefore, that humans took domesticated coyotes to the islands some 6000 years ago. All of this is difficult to prove.

The evidence is stronger for human-assisted introduction of the dingo to Australia and the singing dog to New Guinea. Humans who travelled south from Asia on sailing ships took with them dogs that they had domesticated or semidomesticated. It is thought that the first people to do this were the Austronesians about 4000 to 6000 years ago. The dogs may have been taken onto the ships as food supplies. Evidence suggests that both the dingo and the New Guinea singing dog originated from wolves domesticated in south-eastern Asia, perhaps as recently as 10 000 to 14 000 years ago. In that part of the world, the domestication process selected dogs for food and hunting but, unlike the breeding of dogs in Europe and China, the people in south-eastern Asia did little to change their appearance of the dogs from that of wolves.

In Australia, the dingoes dispersed widely and some believe that this was assisted by Aborigines. The evidence for this is not strong, however, and the dingoes could well have dispersed quite independently of people, just as the red fox did so very much later after it had been introduced to Australia by white settlers. Some dingoes have always lived closely with Aborigines, who related to them as companions, slept with them for warmth at night and also hunted with them. The Aborigines took the dingo pups away from their mothers when they were very young and the women often suckled them. This method of rearing the pups enabled the development of a bond between the dingoes and humans. There are reports that Aborigines sometimes used the dingoes as food but this must have been only when conditions were so harsh that they had little alternative. In fact the first European settlers remarked on the affection that Aborigines had for their dingoes.

The dingoes were isolated from other canids until European settlers arrived with their domestic dogs in the late eighteenth century. Due to this long period of isolation and, seemingly, to the fact that the founding members of Australia's dingo populations were quite few in number, the genetic variation of pure dingoes is quite limited. They have remained almost unchanged in appearance for over 5000 years.

The Falkland Island wolf, the Australian dingo and the New Guinea singing dog are examples of human-assisted spread of dogs in the distant past but this means of dispersal of dogs has continued and is ongoing in the present day. Human-assisted spread of the domestic dog is unrivalled by any other species. The domestic dog now occurs in every part of the world and in all kinds of association with humans, ranging from close membership of human families to pariah dogs living in or near villages to free-living individuals or packs with only rare association with humans or human habitation. As a consequence, domestic dogs far outnumber every other canid species worldwide.

Dingoes and feral dogs

When they first arrived in Australia, European settlers dispersed domestic dogs into the wild both deliberately and by accident. This practice has continued ever since, and it extends to other canid species, as exemplified by the recent introductions of foxes to Tasmania. We call the wild domestic dogs 'feral'. In some parts of the world today, the spread of feral dogs threatens the existence of pure forms of a number of species of wild dogs because they interbreed with them.

This interbreeding is the second major threat to survival faced by dingoes since the arrival of Europeans in Australia. The first was killing by shooting, laying of poisons and trapping. In 1830 the New South Wales government put a bounty on the dingo's head and within the next hundred years around half a million dingo scalps had been submitted for cash payment. The early European settlers of Australia treated the dingo with as much contempt as they did the thylacines (marsupial tigers), which they managed to drive to extinction. The killing of dingoes continues unabated today. When the first Europeans arrived in Australia, the dingo was spread throughout the continent but it did not occur in Tasmania. Now dingoes have been eliminated from much of South Australia, Victoria and New South Wales. The construction of a dog-proof fence almost 6000 kilometres long, extending across South Australia and southern Queensland, followed by extermination programs south of this fence has been the main reason for their decreased numbers. War on dingoes continues sometimes under the 'justification' of protecting stock and other times of protecting the native fauna. At the same time, however, there are moves to save pure-bred dingoes and recognise their importance in Australia's natural history.

It is true that the farming practices of the colonists of Australia led, initially, to a large increase in the dingo population, since food and water became available to them at all times throughout the year and, to some extent, over periods of drought. The additional food came in the form of other recently introduced species, including rabbits and sheep, and water was available at the bores and dams. The 'control' killings that ensued did little more than fragment the packs into smaller groupings, thereby removing the natural controls on breeding, imposed by the alpha female on other females in her pack. As a result, numbers continued to increase and probably peaked from the 1930s to the 1950s. The increased population was largely, if not entirely, made up of purebred dingoes. By the 1960s, however, feral dogs were beginning to infiltrate the breeding dingo population. Since then the number of purebred dingoes has declined so rapidly that Australia's purebred dingoes are predicted to become extinct by the end of the twenty-first century. Already more than half of the remaining dingo population of southern Australia are mainly hybrids of dingoes and feral dogs. The top half of Australia still has mostly purebred dingoes, but hybrids occur increasingly in areas of human population and as roads are made into formerly inaccessible regions.

Contrary to popular belief, dingoes may not be confined to Australia. A type of dingo still occurs in South-East Asia, in Thailand in particular, but these dingoes are now known to be somewhat different from the Australian dingoes and should probably be assigned to a different subspecies. The Thai dingoes are also likely to hybridise with feral dogs as pet dogs become more popular in Asia. Unfortunately, wherever people have pet dogs, some become feral and begin to interbreed with the wild canids. There is no acceptable way of preventing this since no method of killing feral or wild dogs can be selective for one and not the other.

Initially, it might be difficult for a feral dog to be accepted into dingo society and that would act as some barrier to interbreeding. But there are two important points to make about this. The first is that a study found that the majority of dingoes in central Australia are seen alone, so a feral dog may not need to penetrate a strong, exclusive and large group. The second is that the barrier of dingo social life is by no means impenetrable and, once feral dogs have been integrated into dingo society, the barrier to further crossbreeding should become weaker because the resulting behaviour of the hybrid dogs is likely to be less hostile to further integration of feral dogs. In other words, there are predictions that the loss of pure-bred dingoes will proceed at an increasing rate as more feral and hybrid dogs integrate with them.

Although the majority of dingoes seen in central Australia are alone, this does not mean that they lack a coherent social structure. Obviously, they pair to mate and raise their young. They also form groups to hunt or to socialise. In wilderness areas of Australian, such as the Simpson Desert, dingoes live in clans. This suggests that living in clans may be possible only where dingoes are left undisturbed by humans, although other factors such as availability of different types of prey may also be very important in this respect.

Wolves and feral dogs

Without doubt, the first wolves associating with humans would have moved into and out of the wild and would have mixed with wolves that had remained completely separate from humans. In fact, individual wolves would have varied in their degree of contact with humans. In time, the populations of the wolves living in contact with humans would have become separate from the populations of wolves remaining wild. The two populations would have made less and less contact but this did not mean that they had no contact at all. Some interbreeding must always have taken place because some of the dogs living with humans would have become feral. Added to this, wild wolves would have, occasionally, strayed into human camps or villages and bred with the dogs there. Even today there are reports of male grey wolves pairing with domestic dogs and coming back each breeding season to mate with their partner.

Feral dogs are known to interbreed with wolves and this is of considerable concern to conservationists wishing to preserve the remaining populations of grey wolves in Eastern Europe, Italy, Israel, Spain and North America. But a genetic study looking at the extent of hybridisation between feral dogs and grey wolves in Europe found that there has been relatively little interbreeding. It is possible that the behavioural and physiological differences between feral dogs and wolves are too large to permit frequent mating between the species. However, there has been very little research to confirm this hypothesis and different factors may operate for wolves in different populations and regions. For example, the Ethiopian wolf is known to be under threat of extinction to a large extent from hybridisation with feral dogs.

There is no question that wolves and domestic dogs can interbreed but few investigations have been made of how well feral dogs and wolves mix at a social level. In fact, we know relatively little about the behaviour of feral dogs compared to grey wolves and some other canid species.

Domestic dogs can also breed with jackals and coyotes but there are some social barriers that lower the chances of this occurring.

Social behaviour of feral dogs

A study conducted in Italy about a decade ago found that dogs that have quite recently become feral have difficulties in surviving. They suffer from high juvenile mortality and few of them are able to maintain their numbers by reproduction. Instead their numbers are maintained by recruiting more stray domestic dogs. Despite poor survival rates by reproduction, the actual number of feral dogs is increasing. This tells us something about the magnitude of the problems we face to conserve the different species of wild canids. It is also interesting to see how well domestic dogs can adapt to living free of humans.

Humans are an important factor influencing the survival of feral dogs, since they kill them by various means in all parts of the world. Many of the reasons for this persecution of feral dogs are not well substantiated. People believe that that they are highly aggressive and prey predominantly on agricultural animals, thereby reducing farm profits, but there is not a great deal of evidence to support this claim worldwide. The effect of feral dogs on other species depends on exactly what other species are present in their territories. Whereas feral dogs may have little effect on wildlife in Europe, they may have a greater effect in Australia. Also, whereas they may have little effect in one region of Australia, they may have a greater effect in another. It is impossible to generalise, and we are faced with a lack of accurate information in most cases.

The study of feral dogs in Italy found that they were not successful in killing deer or farm animals. Most of them had not become completely independent of humans since they continued to sustain themselves on food provided by humans. Their main source of this food was garbage dumps. This finding was very important because it showed that, contrary to general opinion, the feral dogs in that region were not on the rampage killing livestock and wildlife. In Australia, however, feral dogs may have an important impact on certain endangered birds and small marsupials and, in the Galapagos Islands, turtles, all ground-nesting birds and marine iguanas are at risk from feral dogs. Although feral dogs may have adapted to killing small prey, it appears that they are not successful hunters of larger animals. Their hunting packs for larger animals are often so uncoordinated that they are not successful in bringing down the prey, and they have been observed to bark continually during the hunt, which also lowers their chances of success.

There are another two reasons thought to explain their lack of success in hunting large animals, including live-stock. The first is their lack of opportunity to learn hunting skills from their parents. The second is an absence of consistent leadership in the social group, compared to wolves. The feral dogs' social behaviour can be seen as more flexible or unstable than that of wolves, with their rigid social hierarchies. This means that feral dogs lack the dependable and precise coordination that wild canids employ for successful pack-hunting of large prey. At least, these are the findings from studies in Europe. For one reason or another, the same is not the case in Australia, where the evidence points to a significant impact of feral dogs on sheep.

The social structure of feral dogs also affects their success in breeding. Unlike wolf society, in feral dog clans many pairs breed and while this might seem to lead to more offspring, it is not the case. When conditions are harsh and food is difficult to find, the clan does better by concentrating its efforts on a smaller number of pups and all in the same litter, a strategy developed by wolves and African wild dogs. It seems that feral dogs faced with hardship spread their efforts too thin and so they are less successful in raising young. Added to this, the timing of oestrus in feral dogs is not synchronised, as it is in wolves, and this means that any helper system, by dogs that undergo pseudopregnancies and assist in raising the young of other dogs, fails to occur. Without a helper system, feral dogs with pups must leave them unattended in the den while they go in search of food. Although they might make these forays for feeding as short as possible, it is inevitable that the pups left alone are vulnerable to attack from other members of the pack and from predators. This alone may account for the higher rate of infant mortality in feral dogs compared to wolves. The study conducted in Italy found that not even the paternal dog assisted the mother in rearing her pups.

The clan size of feral dogs is usually smaller than that of wolves, as most studies have reported. Possibly the lack of a rigid social hierarchy leads to fragmentation of larger groups.

The breed of domestic dog from which the feral dogs have been drawn might be very important in determining the behaviour of the feral dog clan. If the domestic breeds contributing to the feral clans retain more wolf-like characteristics, the feral clan may adopt behaviour closer to that of wolves.

However, we should not forget that dogs depend on learning passed on from generation to generation. This applies to knowing how to hunt, find food and water and to care for the young in the wild. The absence of these traditions is a severe limitation to feral dogs. They lack the cultural traditions of wolves and other wild canids. Human intervention in their lifestyle has, in essence, robbed them of their culture.

TEN

The South American bush dog,
speothos venaticus.

Future of the wild dog

Our relationship with wild dogs is extremely contradictory. We love our pet dogs and almost all the behavioural qualities we like best in them are derived from their wild cousin, the grey wolf. The dingo is also very close to the grey wolf and is quite special both for this reason and because it has some special adaptations of its own. Yet, in Australia we have hunted, poisoned and killed them. This destructive attitude is not just a newly acquired one. Indeed, hundreds of years of human expansion and human persecution have brought many canid and other species to the very brink of extinction. When we talk about the future of the wild dog then, we are forced to consider this in the context of widely oppositional practices, attitudes and circumstances.

At the same time that action is being taken to prevent the extinction of certain species of wild canids, debates continue on how to best kill them to prevent them from replenishing their numbers in the next breeding cycle. In practice, both population management and conservation strategies have come across substantial problems and have seen substantial failures. The flaws in efforts to 'manage' wildlife, be this for purposes of conservation or destruction, reverberate all around the world, with similar failures and problems associated with most species in most regions and for most efforts.

One of the contributing factors to the unimpressive record of many kinds of human intervention has to do with the knowledge (or lack of it) and attitudes we bring to a species. All too often management and conservation strategies have displayed ignorance about the behaviour of the animals either to be eliminated or to be saved.

This also applies to attempts to reintroduce endangered species to their natural habitat. For decades, the practice has relied on the assumption that animals act largely on instinct and all we need to do is to raise them in captivity and then release them. The fact is that most animals, certainly mammals and birds, need to learn the art of survival. In the case of canids, they need to learn social skills and the highly skilled art of hunting (see p. 178).

Population management

Control and management of canid populations worldwide is always associated with human expansion and, in particular, with sheep and cattle farming, and sometimes, also with poultry farming. At these junctures human interests and husbandry practices clash with wildlife populations. The concept of canids as a competing species detrimental to human interests, therefore, goes back several thousand years and even then was usually associated with herding and agriculture.

There are three different areas in which encounters with wild dogs have featured as problems. First, there are the inevitable clashes between human expansion and native canid wildlife. This has occurred in the cases of wolves in Eurasia and North America, with the coyote in North America and the various species of canids in South America, India and Africa and fox populations in Europe. Almost anywhere in the world where wild canids occur human populations have contested their living space.

A second group of wild dogs at loggerheads with humans is that introduced by human error or design to parts of the world where they do not belong. This has happened in many parts of the world, including many islands. An example of this problem is the introduction of red foxes into Australia and New Zealand, along with a range of other species of flora and fauna (pigs, rats, goats, cats and rabbits). This practice has caused havoc for native flora and fauna, followed by rapid declines and sometimes extinctions of local species. As a result, the introduced species are largely treated as vermin and usually cannot even muster public support for their humane removal or control.

The dingo takes a peculiar mid-position between these two different standpoints. Dingoes arrived in Australia several thousand years ago and they are regarded either as an introduced scourge or as a native animal. Were it not for the individual, and often private, efforts of some, the dingo would already be extinct in most parts of Australia.

The third problem area is where native wild dogs have too often been confused with feral dogs and borne the brunt of human anger and calls for revenge when livestock have been mauled. Research has shown that feral dogs pose little threat in some parts of the world (see Chapter 9) but, for reasons that are not yet well understood, feral dogs pose a real menace to Australian wildlife and livestock. Laurie Corbett found that one of the problems with feral dogs is associated with the reproductive cycle. A lack of synchrony of the oestrus cycle in feral and hybrid dogs may lead them to kill more often than wild dogs. When packs of wolves, dholes or dingoes attack and kill, they do so to obtain food. This is not the case for many of the kills made by feral dogs studied in Australia: they will attack, maul and savage livestock and then leave it to die without feeding on it. Limiting contact with or inventing ways of suppressing oestrus in hybrids, Corbett argues, would prevent much damage to livestock. Urban groups of unsupervised or poorly supervised domestic dogs are also a threat. When their owners are out (or do not care), they may jump the fence, take to the streets or nearby fields and look for trouble. They

band together roaming sheep farms and mauling sometimes scores of sheep at a time, leaving behind a gruesome
scene of severely injured animals. In the latter case, one
suspects that the motivation for these behaviours derives
from mischief alone, similar to juvenile delinquency.
In the case of the latter, authorities have finally taken one
small step in the right direction insisting that domestic
dogs need to be micro-chipped. At least, when a problem
dog is caught, owners can be held accountable for the
damage that they have caused indirectly.

Dingoes and coyotes will eat young livestock, if they
have access to them, but it has been found that the
marauding dingoes are usually young and inexperienced
and they resort to these domesticated food sources at a
time when they disperse from their natal range. It has
also been found that adult dingoes prefer their normal
diet of kangaroo and other native fare and will take these,
even in preference to calves that are much easier to catch.

The costs and the methods

There is no doubt that predators of domestic livestock
are very costly to individuals and to any economy, irrespective of whether the predators are native or introduced
species. Feral dogs and sometimes dingoes have been
known to take as much as 30 per cent of calves and, in
some regions of Australia and the United States, sheep
farming would be pointless without good measures of
control.

The problem is always dual, since there is a need to keep predators at bay and to keep the numbers of predators down. These are two separate issues and quite often only one or the other has been addressed at any one time. Some strategies have actually had adverse effects overall because of this see-saw approach: reducing predation in one area may increase predator numbers elsewhere, and reducing predators might even increase predation. Methods to keep out predators may be very useful for one particular property or area but not another. For example, electric fencing or predator-proof fencing may be useful but, unless the population is controlled on the other side of that fence, populations of predators there may thrive.

Australia's famous dog-proof fence, stretching nearly 6000 kilometres across Queensland, New South Wales and South Australia, is the most notable single attempt to control predation. The fence is of a length that would stretch from St Petersburg to the Gulf of Aden in the Yemen or almost across the United States from New York to Los Angeles. The costs for just maintaining it are exorbitant (presently about $150 per kilometre annually) but sheep farms could not exist without it. Building fences has of course no effect on predator *numbers* and so, very often, the problem is shifted from domesticated stock which fences protect to native wildlife which may derive no benefit from farm fences. The latter is only a problem in areas where that wildlife has been seriously compromised by other problems. For instance, in Australia, the fox and the rabbit in combination have exerted tremendous pressure on smaller weight-range mammals and additional predation can therefore be problematic.

Predator numbers are also a concern but some methods of 'culling' have actually led to an increase in predator populations. This is very true of coyotes as it is of foxes. A decline in population size may lead to an increase in breeding, replenishing numbers very swiftly. The red fox has also been poisoned or killed in habitats where it is a native species. In these cases, persecution of the red fox has been based on the claim that they are the principle reservoir of the rabies infection. Where red foxes live in close proximity with domestic pets, outbreaks of rabies are particularly difficult to contain, but this is often not the case, even in urban areas where foxes have taken up residence and become scavengers. Urban habitats have become so fragmented that exchanges between fragmented fox populations—a precondition for disease transfers—have become near impossible in some areas and hence the risk to domestic dogs is increasingly exaggerated.

'Management' of fox populations has been largely carried out by using poison baiting with 1080 (sodium fluoroacetate), shooting, trapping and euthanasia, exclusion with fencing and den fumigation. The strategy of poisoning has many undesirable and very controversial side effects. First, almost all acts of poisoning are cruel because they subject the animal to suffering, often to prolonged convulsions and extreme pain. Death does not come in seconds or minutes but may take many hours or even a day. Second, although the target species may be a species that is known to be abundant, such as the intractable coyote or the red fox, the baits may be taken by many other species, including rare native species that may already have a problem with predators. For instance, in 1994 in California alone, almost 2000 coyotes were poisoned, in 1995 well over 1000 were killed, and in 1996 the poison compound 1080 killed nearly 2000 coyotes. These programs of 'management' were considered to be successful. However, in the same three-year period, the poisoning was also proven to have killed nearly thirty domestic dogs, one hundred foxes (red and grey), about fifty racoons, seven opossums, two bobcats, three bears and countless other species, including badgers, crows, ravens, vultures, all birds of prey and porcupines. These figures were not counted in the claimed success.

The United States wildlife departments admit that poisons such as 1080 (sodium fluoroacetate) and sodium cyanide also kill non-target species. In Australia, there has been little public debate on this matter, until recently. This poison has now been banned in most countries but, as was the case with DDT, Australia is one of the last countries to face the challenge. Its supposed safety is questionable. The poison is obtained from a plant that occurs naturally in Western Australia and native animals in these broad regions are usually not affected by it. But this is not the case for much of eastern and northern Australia where the substance is as devastating as it is in other countries. The substance was banned in California because it was proven to have a damaging effect on birds of prey. In Australia, birds of prey are declining in numbers partly because they are exposed to the poison baits or, as in the case of wedge-tailed eagles, feed on carcasses of poisoned dingoes or other wildlife for which there is no enforced requirement of removal. In New Zealand, 1080 was meant to control possum and other introduced populations but it was suspected of also killing the endangered national symbol, the kiwi.

Moreover, in California tax payers paid over $3 million per annum for the coyote baiting programs and the outcome, just two years later, was that the coyote population had regained its former population size. One could hardly be criticised for thinking that this 'management' strategy had been cruel, inefficient, money-wasting and destructive. And yet, usually for political expediency, such programs are repeated all over the world, over and over again.

There are other consequences of the haphazard ways of 'controlling' populations of wild dogs that are rarely raised. We have described the close-knit structure and the complexity of wild-dog life in some detail. Yet proponents of indiscriminate killing sprees are usually not aware that, apart from serious ethical considerations, there are lingering impacts on the species in terms of family stability, territorial behaviour and many other concrete biological variables. These too may constitute major costs. We may be changing the very essence of wolves and other wild dogs. We may, by our unethical and inconsistent methods, give rise to far more vicious, dangerous and marauding predators.

In some countries wolves are 'harvested' annually at a very high and often indiscriminate rate. For instance, killing the dominant dog has a major impact on the group, not just in wolves but also in African wild dogs, dholes and any other group-living dog. Leaderless groups cause much more damage than groups under the guidance of an experienced alpha animal. Taking away a dominant dog also disrupts the means by which the social group passes on information for survival from generation to generation. In the generations following the loss of an alpha and other members of the group, we may see behavioural deficiencies and anomalies, as we also see in humans when generation after generation is subjected to ongoing warfare punctuated by deaths in families.

Alternatively, these 'programs' and drives to 'control' populations may also drive species to extinction. This has been happening now for decades and many canid species are under severe threat or endangered. There are anomalies in management practices. For instance, at the very same time as country-wide programs in the United States against coyotes and wolves blossomed (they can still be trapped and shot, even in national parks in Alaska), the work to bring back the red wolf occupied major research and breeding programs. The plight of the red wolf in the United States was recognised in the early 1960s and the species is slowly being hauled back from the brink of extinction by captive breeding programs. In 1976, seventeen red wolves were captured and twenty years later the various zoological breeding programs had raised the number to over two hundred. In 1987 programs to restore them to the wild started. While the red wolf story is a success story in terms of some rehabilitation success, it has had countless pitfalls. Many wolves released into the wild did not survive even for a year, captive-born juveniles released together with parents perished as well and many had to be recaptured and re-released. Pups that were born in the wild lasted for two years, hence considerably longer than those derived from captivity (whether young or adult). In one release, only three wolves, who had been released with their parents, were still alive after five years (just 10 per cent of the released animals) and the oldest survivor was just over six years old at last count. This shows how very difficult such success is won. Captivity selects out different behavioural qualities than are needed in the wild. Moreover, many wolves suffered the same fate as their ancestors: they were shot, poisoned or trapped in national parks. There is no doubt that wild dogs have few friends and that people are their most powerful enemy against whom they have very few defences.

Many alternative programs have been proposed but nearly all of the alternatives are in experimental stages and in their infancy either because governments lack the political will to implement them or because they come under pressure to demonstrate fast and 'decisive' actions and revert back to the old and ineffective ways.

The alternative non-lethal means of controlling wild dogs are manifold and they are directed at both facets of the problem, that of predation and of predator numbers. The difference between the typical old method (poisoning and shooting) and possible alternatives is that poisoning is simple to administer and a singular activity. The old methods have immediate, short-term gain while alternative methods tend to be long term. Alternative methods of control may require the collaboration and simultaneous application of a large variety of strategies and such integrated approaches often appear too cumbersome and politically unattractive, because they cannot provide the same kind of kudos as singular actions often do. Some farmers understandably also want action now rather than drawn-out experimentation. On the other hand, public attitude has favoured more humane methods for at least the last twenty years.

To control predation, physical and electric barriers, as well as deterrents by sound and light, have had some success but these methods of control are not always feasible on very large land holdings. Guard dogs can be used to lower predation on sheep, as can, strangely enough, llamas and donkeys. There are other ways to lower predation, such as using taste aversion (effective in small numbers) that involves lacing a carcass with a non-lethal aversive substance. Prey avoidance, particularly by inexperienced animals, can have long-lasting, even lifelong impact. Electronic dog-training collars have been tested and found to have prevented all attempted attacks on lambs by coyotes for up to four months. This aversive conditioning also holds some promise. Further, diversionary (minimal) feeding at times of crashing natural prey species (such as during times of drought) is another method that appears to have some merit.

Another problem concerns modern husbandry techniques of dehorning, removing older adults and most of the males from a herd. Without horns and additional males, the cattle cannot defend themselves or their calves against dingoes. These techniques leave cattle helpless vis-à-vis the dingo and on very large properties, as in outback Australia, other strategies could be attempted but have not been tried at any sustained level. A strategy used by wild prey animals is to calve together. It is feasible to learn from other animals' self-defences and recreate the well-tried practices of wild ungulates (deer, impala, gazelles, sambar) on cattle in such outback places. Herding them together for calving, allowing more males in and allowing them to keep their horns should reduce predation in situations where it is difficult to supervise stock or protect it by fencing.

None of these methods alone is affecting the population size of the predators directly but a two-pronged approach addresses predator success and predator populations at the same time. One particularly humane and sensible way to reduce predator population size is to reduce fertility. In this way, territories do not change hands, the predator population remains stable and cannot respond to an increase in food supply. Over a period of time, a successful, fully integrated program of this kind will gradually reduce the population to a *stable* level, thereby reducing predation on domestic stock and, in conjunction with other methods of predator deterrence, as described, the dogs are then forced back to search for their natural range of prey. This method has not gained overwhelming support or research dollars in the past because it seems to be unattractively slow in achieving a desired result.

However, it is well to remember that the allegedly 'decisive' acts of poisoning and shooting that claim some short-term victories have not had any noteworthy long-term effects on predator numbers or incidence of livestock losses, let alone on permanent alleviation of predator problems. One could equally argue that failure to have seriously studied, tested and applied possibly effective alternative long-term strategies has been culpably and inexcusably negligent. Valuable time and opportunities have been wasted. Enormous sums of money have been squandered on short-term remedies without bringing about any real long-term solutions. Moreover, killing may have long-term effects on the behaviour of the surviving predators to the detriment of domesticated stock and native wildlife.

In many instances, our notion that predator species ought to be removed completely may also have serious environmental consequences. Martyn Gorman, vice chairman of the UK Mammal Society, told a surprised audience in 1999 at the British Association's Festival of Science in Sheffield that he would favour the reintroduction of the Scottish wolf into the Highlands because of the explosion of deer numbers in Scotland. Deer, despite increased 'culling', were multiplying at an alarming rate and doing substantial damage. Scotland then had an estimated 350 000 deer and they were destroying young trees, shrubs, and indeed almost any growth of any kind. The obvious advantage of natural predators is that the predator–prey relationship has some inbuilt insurances for the health and long-term survival of both.

There is another poorly managed issue that involves consideration of food sources for predator species. For instance, in 2002 there were headlines and controversies in Victoria, Australia, that 15 000 kangaroos had been shot in a very brief span of time. Some of the animals were apparently starving because of drought conditions. Actions of this kind, whether justified in specific cases or not, rarely take into account the broader ecological effects. The sudden disappearance of a substantial food source can have a major impact on predators that naturally prey or feed on 'culled' animals. Where will they find their next meal? And what will be done when hungry dingoes suddenly appear at town edges or on farms looking for alternative food? While this extraordinary act may shock because of its wilfulness and malice, it is certainly not unique. Most acts of wildlife 'control' are acts done in isolation without any insight into the total effect (and many undesirable side effects) and without any under-standing or sense of needing to integrate information of the wider circumstances and possible behavioural consequences.

Conservation

Unfortunately, perhaps as many as about 80 per cent of all rehabilitation and reintroduction projects for threat-ened species in the last 50 years have more or less failed (be this for birds, sea mammals, primates, large cats or wild dogs) because the most dedicated and devoted teams of researchers and wildlife managers rarely have any formal training and understanding of animal behaviour. Biology, zoology, veterinary science and ecology are all highly useful disciplines to bring to bear on any manage-ment and conservation program of wildlife or introduced species but usually the area of knowledge missing in these endeavours is ethology (animal behaviour). So appalling is the state of affairs that the prestigious journal *Nature* published an article in 2001 in which the failure of conser-vation programs was blamed on ignorance about the behaviour of the species being protected from extinction.

Repeatedly groups of animals have been released into the wild only to meet their end, and this applies to other species as well as dogs. For instance, eighty gibbons that were released in South-East Asia in the 1980s all starved to death within a few months, and of sixty koalas released in Australia in the 1990s none survived for more than half a year. The individual gibbons released had not been taught in detail how to recognise food and where to find it. In the case of the koalas, they had not been taught predator recognition. In the case of wolf releases, lack of success may be associated with a failure to teach them to fear humans and so they become easy targets for hunters.

A particularly tragic case, involving dingoes and human contact, occurred on Australia's Fraser Island in 2001. On this island, the wild dingoes not only lived in close proximity to humans but tourists were not actively controlled or dissuaded from approaching them. In fact, some tourist operators fed the dingoes so that tourists could have their photographs taken with them. The wildlife managers appear to have lacked understanding that a 'wild' dog is a carnivore and, like all carnivores of the size of a dog or more, they are potentially dangerous to humans.

Fear of humans is the only protection we have from a variety of carnivorous species. To take it away is to invite problems. When, in the case of Fraser Island, a child was killed by a dingo, many other dingoes were shot as a consequence. The dingoes should never have been killed but nor should they have been encouraged to mix with humans. Today, the modern term for 'killing' is 'culling' but the practice is the same. Forty dingoes had already been shot on Fraser Island before the fatal attack. Indeed, every time a dingo showed 'aggressive' behaviour, it was seen as a justifiable excuse to destroy it. But dingoes are hunters so their behaviour to attack, dispel or feed on a victim is prey behaviour, not aggression. Lions in Krüger National Park have killed humans when they have stepped out of their cars against explicit instructions but no one would seriously entertain the idea of shooting every lion in the vicinity of the attack. Because dingoes look so much like our favourite house pet, it is perhaps easy to forget that they are carnivores. Fear is the only method to keep them at safe distances from humans but this is precisely what tourists and tour operators alike, very wrongfully, tried to train out of the dingoes of Fraser Island.

Wild dogs simply do not attack humans unless humans have set the scene for this to occur. One of the most efficient killers amongst carnivores is the African wild dog but, in Zimbabwe and on the open plains of Serengeti, there has been no single incident recorded in myth, legend or fact of a dog attacking a human.

To an ethologist, these tragedies described are all very predictable outcomes but, to this day, the importance of understanding animal behaviour—a science in itself—is not fully appreciated or utilised in the overwhelming majority of conservation programs. Ultimately, it is behaviour that will make animals either survive or succumb. Unless they know and recognise their own kind and understand the etiquettes of their species, and unless they know how and what to eat, where to find it and in which season, how to spot and recognise potential enemies or predators and what techniques to use in case of an attack, there is little hope of any success. For the animal, it is vital to have these skills and abilities and be able to use them instantly.

Detailed knowledge of the behaviour of wild dogs will ultimately contribute to re-establishing them or controlling them humanely, and positively, in areas and regions where they are currently perceived as pests. Knowledge of animal behaviour means being able, after systematic study, to predict what an animal will choose to do in certain situations and under certain ecological conditions.

There are many excellent wild-dog experts who have very detailed knowledge of dog behaviour but conservation or reintroductory programs, like those for population and predation control, are too often in the hands of government agencies that, even after obtaining this knowledge, base their decisions on short-term solutions for ideological reasons. The same government agencies, at times seriously underqualified to make the decisions they do, then claim that systems of introduction or conservation have not worked. It is at that point that they often choose to argue that rehabilitation is a failure or that management requires using poisons or mounting large shooting parties. Lack of homework and the need for expediency by these decision-makers sets up a vicious cycle.

Moreover, some of the criteria for successful conservation are very different in different habitats. African wild dogs are vulnerable because of predator competition; dholes, however, do not appear to have this problem, at least not of the same magnitude. It has been found that social dominance between species, of crucial importance in the savannah habitats of the African wild dog, might play a relatively minor role in other habitats. Tiger, leopard and dhole live in the same environment with overlapping prey species and, the occasional chase and killing of each other not withstanding, manage to coexist, so that a wildlife refuge continues to work well also for dholes. But the same concept—of providing a refuge for predator and prey populations—when applied to the open plains in Africa, may ultimately doom the African wild dog. For dholes, ecological factors, such as adequate availability of appropriate-sized prey, dense cover and high tree densities, may be the primary factors to consider for their conservation.

Finally, one additional problem in dealing with endangered species, and wild dogs in particular, concerns the maintenance of genetic diversity and, at the same time, the maintenance of the species. Interbreeding with domestic and domestic feral dogs is now a cause for the decline of certain canids, chief among them being the Australian dingo, the Ethiopian wolf and, in some parts, the grey wolf.

Conservation parks and the ranges of wild dogs

Not all canids have well-defined territories, especially not outside the breeding season. Yet it is very important for effective conservation, and even for the management of wild dogs in areas in which they are regarded as pests, to know their territorial boundaries or use of denning areas. For instance, we need to know how dispersal occurs in parks in which they are protected. Unfortunately, much evidence shows that some or many of these parks are too small for the wild dogs. Wolves move in and out of parks during winter to follow migratory deer. As a result, many wolves, when outside the parks, are shot by humans and these senseless killings often involve dominant pairs, central to the clan.

A review of worldwide park systems in 1981 suggested that only 22 per cent of parks are likely to sustain their large carnivore inhabitants over the next one hundred years. There are additional problems that will need to be addressed if wild dog populations are to find a secure haven. Parks are often not set up to accommodate and account for preferences in denning areas (near water or cliffs), so the wild dog pair goes in search of a suitable place, often located outside the park. Many of these dens get reused and frequented by other clan members and so there is the added risk that major survival activities, such as breeding, take place outside park boundaries. Since the legislative power of park managers and agencies may be limited, they are helpless to act in preventing further killings of species outside park boundaries. In fact, parks tend to attract hunters to their surrounding regions because they are well aware that the animals will not necessarily know the boundaries of the park.

The concept of national parks, once thought to be an obvious solution to the problem of survival of all species, has major flaws. Artificial borders are not known or respected by animals. If the borders hold but the park is too small, the numbers of certain species will reduce over time. This can disturb the delicate equilibrium between predators and prey and lead to overcrowding of the park by other species. Some important amendments have been made in some regions of the world, including Australia, to address the problems of park size by establishing corridors between parks to create linkage systems that enable some traffic between various protected regions and minimise the worst effects of isolation and fragmentation.

Our human attempts to recreate 'natural' conditions by merely declaring an area protected have been extraordinarily naive. For instance, in Krüger National Park animals are culled regularly and their parts are sold as trophies to an eager tourist market. There may be good reason to do this (to discourage poachers and all manner of illegal trade) but it proves that these environments do not achieve an ecological equilibrium, or sustainable balance of predator species. African wild dogs, under natural conditions, rarely get killed by lions, but in national parks they do. Research has established that clans of African wild dogs need a minimum of five individuals to remain viable. Trade-offs between hunting and pup-guarding mean that in a small clan fewer dogs bring back less food to individuals at the den. If we factor in predator competition at food sites (such as jackals, hyenas and lions) the minimum size of five per clan seems to be far too small—clans of African wild dogs used to be made up of hundreds of dogs, presumably for a good reason.

Further, the sanctity of national parks everywhere continues to be under threat. Mining in Kakadu National Park, in Australia, or the plans of the United States government to exploit oil resources right in the midst of one of the most unusual Arctic refuges in north-east Alaska, despite bitter opposition in 2002 by the US Natural Resources Defence Council, exemplify the willingness of some to disregard the many warning signs about the fragile health of this planet. Wild dogs are a very good indication of that fragility, especially those living in groups.

Tragically, the demise of wild dogs is greatest the more closely their lifestyle resembles that of human society. The larger group-living, stable family groups with strong commitments to each other are those that are endangered. The more solitary species such as the fox or the coyote, who have learned to adapt to human presence and can get by with scavenging and lone hunting forays, are the species that thrive.

The domestic dog is one of the most successful single species in terms of cohabitation with humans. There are statues to dogs all over the world. These statues attest to the bravery, devotion and loyalty of dogs. We are privileged to share their company. We should feel equally privileged to share our world with wild dogs.

APPENDIX

The classification of Canidae

Genus	Species	Common names
Canis	*lupus*	grey wolf
	rufus	red wolf
	simensis	Ethiopian wolf or Simien jackal
	aureus	golden jackal or Asiatic jackal
	mesomelas	black-backed jackal or silver-backed jackal
	adustus	side-striped jackal
	latrans	coyote, prairie wolf or brush wolf
	familiaris (or lupus) dingo	dingo
	familiaris (or lupus) hallstromi	New Guinea singing dog
	familiaris domesticus	dog or domestic dog

Genus	Species	Common names
Vulpes	*vulpes*	red fox
	pallida	pale fox, pallid fox or African sand fox
	chama	Cape fox, Kama fox or silver 'jackal'
	bengalensis	Bengal fox or Indian fox
	rueppelli	Rüppell's fox or sand fox
	cana	Blanford's fox or Afghan fox
	corsac	Steppe fox or Corsac fox
	ferrilata	Tibetan fox or Tibetan sand fox
	velox	kit fox, swift fox or prairie fox
Urocyon	*cinereoargenteus*	grey fox or tree-climbing fox
	littoralis	island fox
Fennecus	*zerda*	fennec fox
Otocyon	*megalotis*	bat-eared fox, black-eared fox or Delande's fox
Alopex	*lagopus*	Arctic fox
Dusicyon (also *Pseudalopex*)	*culpaeus*	culpeo or Santa Helena zorro*
	griseus	grey zorro, Argentine grey fox or chilla

The classification of Canidae

Genus	Species	Common names
	gymnocerus	pampas fox or Azara's zorro
	sechurae	Sechuran fox, Sechuran zorro
Dusicyon (also *Atelocynus*)	*microtis*	small-eared zorro
Dusicyon (also *Lycalopex*)	*vetulus*	hoary zorro, hoary fox or small-toothed dog
Cerdocyon	*thous*	crab-eating zorro
Speothos	*venaticus*	bush dog or vinegar dog
Lycaon	*pictus*	African wild dog, Cape hunting dog, African hunting dog or African painted dog
Cuon	*alpinus*	dhole, Asiatic wild dog or whistling hunter
Chrysocyon	*brachyurus*	maned wolf
Nyctereutes	*procyonoides*	raccoon dog

* 'zorro' is the common name for 'fox' in South American species

Note that the Falkland Island wolf (*Dusicyon autralis*), also known as the Antartic wolf or warrah, is not listed since it is extinct.

Selected reading

Chapter 1   The wild dog family

Alderton, D. (1998) *Foxes and Wild Dogs of the World*. Blanford, London.

Coppinger, R. and Coppinger, L. (2001) *Dogs: A Startling New Understanding of Canine Origin, Behavior, and Evolution*. Scribner, New York.

Palmqvist, P., Arribas, A. and Martinez-Navarro, B. (1999) Eco-morphological study of large canids of the lower Pleistocene of southeastern Spain. *Lethaia*, 32, 75–88.

Reich, D.E., Wayne, R.K. and Goldstein, D.B. (1999) Genetic evidence for a recent origin by hybridisation of red wolves. *Molecular Ecology*, 8, 139–44.

Roy, M.S., Geffen, E., Smith, D., Ostrander, E.A. and Wayne, R.K. (1994) Patterns of differentiation and hybridisation in North American wolflike canids, revealed by analysis of microsatellite loci. *Molecular Biology and Evolution*, 11, 553–70.

Ruvinsky, A. and Sampson, J. (2001) *The Genetics of the Dog*. CABI Publishing, Wallingford.

Schwartz, M. (1997) *A History of Dogs in the Early Americas*. Yale University Press, New Haven.

Selected reading

Vila, C., Maldonado, J.E. and Wayne, R.K. (1999) Phylogenetic relationships, evolution, and genetic diversity of the domestic dog. *Journal of Heredity*, 90, 71–7.

Vila, C., Savolainen, P., Maldonado, J.E., Amorin, I.R., Rice, J.E., Honeycutt, R.L., Crandall, K.A., Lundeberg, J. and Wayne, R.K. (1997) Multiple ancient origins of the domestic dog. *Science*, 276, 1687–9.

Wayne, R.K. and Gittleman, J.L. (1995) The problematic red wolf. *Scientific American*, 273, 26–31.

Wayne, R.K. and Jenks, S. (1991) Mitochondrial DNA analysis implying extensive hybridisation of the endangered red wolf, *Canis rufus*. *Nature*, 351, 565–8.

Wayne, R.K. and Ostrander, E.A. (1999) Origin, genetic diversity, and genome structure of the domestic dog. *Bioessays*, 21, 247–57.

Wilson, P.J., Grewal, S., Lawford, I.D., Heal, J.N.M., Granacki, A.G., Pennock, D., Theberge, J.B., Theberge, M.T., Voigt, D.R., Waddell, W., Chambers, R.E., Paquet, P.C., Goulet, G., Cluff, D. and White, B.N. (2000) DNA profiles of the eastern Canadian wolf and the red wolf provide evidence for a common evolutionary history independent of the gray wolf. *Canadian Journal of Zoology*, 78, 2156–66.

Chapter 2 Habitats of the wild dog

Alderton, D. (1998) *Foxes and Wild Dogs of the World*. Blanford, London.

Ballard, W.B., Ayres, L.A., Krausman, P.R., Reed, D.J. and Fancy, S.G. (1997) Ecology of wolves in relation to a migratory caribou herd in Northwest Alaska. *Wildlife Monographs*, 135, 6–47.

Bueler, L.E. (1973) *Wild Dogs of the World*. Stein and Day Publishers, New York.

Corbett, L.K. (1985) Morphological comparisons of Australian and Thai dingoes: a reappraisal of dingo status, distribution and ancestry. *Proceedings of the Ecological Society of Australia*, 13, 277–91.

Dye, C. (1996) Serengeti wild dogs: what really happened? *Trends in Ecology and Evolution*, 11, 188–9. See also comments on pp. 337, 509.

Fleming, P., Corbett, L. Harden, R. and Thomson, P. (2001) *Managing the Impacts of Dingoes and Other Wild Dogs*. Bureau of Rural Sciences, Canberra.

Fox, M. W. (1984) *The Whistling Hunters. Field Studies of the Asiatic Wild Dog* (Cuon Alpinus). State University of New York Press, Albany, NY.

Garciamoreno, J., Matocq, M.D., Roy, M.S., Geffen, E. and Wayne, R.K. (1996) Relationships and genetic purity of the endangered Mexican wolf based on analysis of microsatellite loci. *Conservation Biology*, 10, 376–89.

Ginsberg, J. (1992) Mapping Wild Dogs. *http://www.157.pair.com/ speothos/PUBLICAT/CNDNEWS1/afrwldog.htm.*

Girman, D.J., Wayne, R.K., Kat, P.W., Mills, M.G.L., Ginsberg, J.R., Borner, M., Wilson, V., Fanshawe, J.H., Fitzgibbon, C. and Lau, L.M. (1993) Molecular genetic and morphological analyses of the African wild dog (*Lycaon pictus*). *Journal of Heredity*, 8, 450–9.

Gottelli, D., Sillero-Zubiri, C., Applebaum, G.D., Roy, M.S., Girman, D.J., Garciá-Moreno, J., Ostrander, E.A. and Wayne, R.K. (1994) Molecular genetics of the most endangered canid: the Ethiopian wolf, *Canis simenis. Molecular Ecology*, 3, 301–12.

Hayes, R.D. and Harestad, A.S. (2000) Demography of a recovering wolf population in the Yukon. *Canadian Journal of Zoology*, 78, 36–48.

Kamler, J.F. and Gipson, P.S. (2000) Space and habitat use by resident and transient coyotes. *Canadian Journal of Zoology*, 78, 2106–11.

Kitchen, A.M., Gese, E.M. and Schauster, E.R. (2000) Long-term spatial stability of coyotes (*Canis latrans*) home ranges in southern Colorado. *Canadian Journal of Zoology*, 78, 458–64.

Mercure, A., Ralls, K., Koepfli, K.P. and Wayne, R.K. (1993) Genetic subdivisions among small canids: mitochondrial DNA differentiation of swift, kit, and arctic foxes. *Evolution*, 47, 1313–28.

Selected reading

Mills, M.G.L. and Gorman, M.L. (1997) Factors affecting the density and distribution of wild dogs in the Krüger National Park. *Conservation Biology* 11, 1397–406.

Newsome, A.E., Corbett, L.K. and Carpenter, S.M. (1980) The identity of the dingo. I. Morphological discriminants of dingo and dogs skulls. *Australian Journal of Zoology*, 28, 615–25.

Nowak, R.M. (1995) Walker's Mammals of the World Online. The Johns Hopkins University Press. *http://www.press.jhu.edu/books/walker*.

Roemer, G.W., Smith, D.A., Garcelon, D.K. and Wayne, R.K. (2001) The behavioural ecology of the island fox (*Urocyon littoralis*). *Journal of Zoology*, 255, 1–14.

Schwartz, M. (1997) *A History of Dogs in the Early Americas*. Yale University Press, New Haven.

Vanvalkenburgh, B. and Wayne, R.K. (1994) Shape divergence associated with size convergence in sympatric east African jackals. *Ecology*, 75, 1567–81.

Vila, C., Amorim, I.R., Leonard, J.A., Posada, D., Castroviejo, J., Petrucci-Fonseca, F., Crandall, K.A., Ellegren, H. and Wayne, R.K. (1999) Mitochondrial DNA phylogeography and population history of the grey wolf. *Molecular Ecology*, 8, 2089–103.

Vucetich, J.A. and Creel, S. (1999) Ecological interactions, social organization, and extinction risk in African wild dogs. *Conservation Biology*, 13, 1172–82.

Woodroofe, R. and Ginsberg, J.R. (1999) Conserving the African wild dog *Lycaon pictus*. 1. Diagnosing and treating causes of decline. *Oryx*, 33, 132–42.

Yahnke, C.J., Johnson, W.E., Geffen, E., Smith, D., Hertel, F., Roy, M.S., Bonacic, C.F., Fuller, T.K., Vanvalkenburgh, B. and Wayne, R.K. (1996) Darwin's fox—A distinct endangered species in a vanishing habitat. *Conservation Biology*, 10, 366–75.

Chapter 3   Sensory abilities

Aquino, R. and Puertas, P. (1997) Observations of *Spethos venaticus* (Canidae: Carnivora) in its natural habitat in Peruvian Amazonia.

Zeitschrift für Säugetierkinde (International Journal of Mammalian Biology), 62, 117–18.

Bekoff, M. (2001) Observations of scent-marking and discriminating self from others by a domestic dog (Canis familiaris): tales of displaced yellow snow. Behavioural Processes, 55, 75–9.

Budiansky, S. (2000) The Truth About Dogs. Penguin Books, New York.

Fogle, B. (1990) The Dog's Mind. Pelham Books, London.

Grantiz, U. (1994) Decreased vision and blindness in dogs: A retrospective study. Berliner und Münchener Tierärztliche Wochenschrift, 107, 295–9.

Hepper, P.G. (1994) Long-term retention of kinship recognition established during infancy in the domestic dog. Behavioural Processes, 33, 3–14.

Hirai, T., Kojima, S., Shimada, A., Uemura, T., Sakai, M. and Itakura, C. (1996) Age-related changes in the olfactory system of dogs. Neuropathology and Applied Neurobiology, 22, 531–9.

Miller, P.E. and Murphy, C.J. (1995) Vision in dogs. Journal of the American Veterinary Medical Association, 207, 1623–34.

Millot, J.L. (1994) Olfactory and visual cues in the interaction systems between dogs and children. Behavioural Processes, 33, 177–88.

Neitz, J., Geist, T. and Jacobs, G.H. (1989) Color vision in the dog. Visual Neuroscience, 3, 119–125.

Peichl, L. (1992) Topography of ganglion cells in the dog and wolf retina. Journal of Comparative Neurology, 324, 603–20.

Settle, R.H., Sommerville, B.A., McCormick, J. and Broom, D.M. (1994) Human scent matching using specially trained dogs. Animal Behaviour, 48, 1443–8.

Sommerville, B.A. and Broom, D.M. (1998) Olfactory awareness. Applied Animal Behaviour Science, 57, 269–86.

Thesen, A., Steen, J.B. and Doving, K.B. (1993) Behaviour of dogs during olfactory tracking. Journal of Experimental Biology, 180, 247–51.

Windberg, L.A. (1996) Coyote responses to visual and olfactory stimuli related to familiarity with an area. Canadian Journal of Zoology, 74, 2248–53.

Selected reading

Chapter 4 Communication

Brady, C.A. (1981) The vocal repertoire of the bush dog (*Speothos venaticus*), crab-eating fox (*Cerdocyon thous*), and maned wolf (*Chrysocyon brachyurus*). *Animal Behaviour*, 29, 649–69.

Cohen, J.A. and M.W. Fox (1976) Vocalizations in wild canids and possible effects of domestication. *Behavioural Processes*, 1, 77–92.

Coscia, E.M., Phillips, D.P. and Fentress, J.C. (1991) Spectral analysis of neonatal wolf *Canis lupus* vocalizations. *Bioacoustics*, 3, 275–93.

Durbin, L.S. (1998) Individuality in the whistle call of the Asiatic wild dog *Cuon alpinus*. *Bioacoustics*, 9, 197–206.

Feddersen-Petersen, D.U. (2000) Vocalization of European wolves (*Canis lupus lupus* L.) and various dog breeds (*Canis lupus* f.fam.) *Arch. Tierz. Drummerstorf*, 43, 387–97.

Fox, M.W. (1969) A comparative study of the development of facial expression in canids: wolf, coyote and foxes. *Behaviour*, 36, 4–73.

Fox, M. W. (1971) *Behaviour of Wolves, Dogs and Related Canids*. Jonathan Cape, London.

Fox, M. W. (1971) Socio-infantile and socio-sexual signals in canids: a comparative and ontogenetic study. *Zeitschrift für Tierpsychologie*, 28, 185–210.

Fox, M. W. (1978) *The Dog: Its Domestication and Behavior*. Garland STPM Press, New York.

Fox, M. W. (1984) *The Whistling Hunters. Field Studies of the Asiatic Wild Dog (Cuon Alpinus)*. State University of New York Press, Albany, NY.

Frommolt, K.H., Kaal, M.I. Paschina, N.M. and Nikolskij, A.A. (1988) Sound development of the wolf (*Canis lupus* L., Canidae L.). *Zool. Jahrbuch Physiol.* 92, 105–15.

Goddard, M.E. and Beilharz, R.G. (1985) Individual variation in agonistic behaviour in dogs. *Animal Behaviour*, 33, 1338–42.

Harrington, F.H. (1987) Aggressive howling in wolves. *Animal Behaviour*, 35, 7–12.

Henry, J.D. (1977) The use of urine marking in the scavenging behaviour of the red fox (*Vulpes vulpes*). *Behaviour*, 61, 82–105.

Kappe, T. (1996) Subjective resource value and the intensity of threat vocalizations in European wolves (*Canis lupus lupus*). *Proceedings* of the 1st International Symposium on Physiology and Ethology of Wild and Zoo Animals, Supplement II, 97–100.

Kleiman, D.G. (1967) Some aspects of social behaviour in the Canidae. American Zoologist, 7, 365–72.

Lopez, B.H. (1978) Of Wolves and Men. Charles Scribner's Sons, New York.

Marler, P. and W. J.I. Hamilton (1966) Mechanisms of Animal Behavior. John Wiley and Sons, New York.

McCarley, H. (1978) Vocalizations of red wolves. Journal of Mammalogy, 59, 27–35.

McConnell, P.B. (1990) Acoustic structure and receiver response in domestic dogs, Canis familiaris. Animal Behaviour 39, 897–904.

Mech, D.L. (1970) The Wolf: The Ecology and Behavior of an Endangered Species. The Natural History Press, Garden City, N.Y.

Morton, E.S. (1977) On the occurrence and significance of motivation–structural rules in some bird and mammal sounds. American Naturalist, 111, 855–69.

Newton-Fisher, S.H., White, P. and Jones, G. (1993) Structure and function of red fox Vulpes vulpes vocalisations. Bioacoustics, 5, 1–31.

Nowak, R.M. (1995) Walker's Mammals of the World Online. The Johns Hopkins University Press. http://www.press.jhu.edu/books/walker.

Peters, R.P. and D.L. Mech (1975) Scent-marking in wolves. American Scientist, 63, 629–37.

Robbins, R.L. (2000) Vocal communication in free-ranging African wild dogs (Lycaon pictus). Behaviour, 137, 1271–98.

Robbins, R.L. and McCreery, K.E. (2000) Dominant female cannibalism in the African wild dog. African Journal of Ecology, 38, 91–2.

Rogers, L.J. and Kaplan, G. (1998) Not Only Roars and Rituals. Allen & Unwin, Sydney.

Rothman, R.J. and D.L. Mech (1979) Scent-marking in lone wolves and newly formed pairs. Animal Behaviour, 27, 750–60.

Schassburger, R. (1993) Vocal Communication in the Timber Wolf, Canis lupus, Linnaeus. Structure, Motivation, and Ontogeny. Paul Parey Scientific Publishers, Berlin.

Selected reading

Shalter, M.D., Fentress, J.C. and Young, G.W. (1976) Determinants of response of wolf pups to auditory signals. *Behaviour*, 60, 98–114.

Tooze, Z.J., Harrington, F.H. and Fentress, J.C. (1990) Individually distinct vocalizations in timber wolves, *Canis lupus*. *Animal Behaviour*, 40, 723–30.

Well, M.C. and Bekoff, M. (1981) An observational study of scent-marking in coyotes (*Canis latrans*). *Animal Behaviour*, 29, 332–50.

Chapter 5 Social life

Biben, M. (1983) Comparative ontogeny of social behaviour in three South American canids, the maned wolf, crab-eating fox and bushdog: implications for sociality. *Animal Behaviour*, 31, 814–26.

Fox, M. W. (1971) Socio-infantile and socio-sexual signals in canids: a comparative and ontogenetic study. *Zeitschrift für Tierpsychologie*, 28, 185–210.

Fox, M. W. (1984) *The Whistling Hunters. Field Studies of the Asiatic Wild Dog* (Cuon Alpinus*). State University of New York Press, Albany, NY.

Frommolt, K.H., Kaal, M.I. Paschina, N.M. and Nikolskij, A.A. (1988) Sound development of the wolf (*Canis lupus* L., Canidae L.). *Zool. Jahrbuch Physiologie*, 92, 105–15.

Johnsingh, A.J.T. (1982) Reproductive and social behaviour of the Dhole, *Cuon alpinus* Canidae). *Journal of Zoology, London*, 198, 443–63.

Lorenz, Konrad (1979) *Man Meets Dog*, Methuen & Co, London.

MacDonald, D.W. and Courtenay, O. (1996) Enduring social relationships in a population of crab-eating zorros, *Cerdocyon thous*, in Amazonian Brazil (Carnivora, Canidae). *Journal of Zoology, London*, 239, 329–55.

McNutt, J.W. (1996) Sex-biased dispersal in African wild dogs, *Lycaon pictus*. *Animal Behaviour*, 52, 1067–77.

Schassburger, R. (1993) *Vocal Communication in the Timber Wolf,* Canis lupus, *Linnaeus. Structure, Motivation, and Ontogeny.* Paul Parey Scientific Publishers, Berlin.

Schenkel, R. (1967) Submission: its features and function in the wolf and dog. *American Zoologist,* 7, 319–29.

Zabel, C.J. and Taggart, S.J. (1989) Shift in red fox, *Vulpes vulpes,* mating system associated with El Niño in the Bering Sea. *Animal Behaviour,* 38, 830–8.

Chapter 6   Sex and reproduction

Asa, C.S. and Valdespino, C. (1998) Canid reproductive biology: an integration of proximate mechanisms and ultimate causes. *American Zoologist,* 38, 251–9.

Creel, S., Creel, N.M. and Monfort, S.L. (1998) Birth order, estrogens and sex-ratio adaptation in African wild dogs (*Lycaon pictus*). *Animal Reproduction Science,* 53, 315–20.

Creel, S., Creel, N.M., Mills, M. and Monfort, S.L. (1997) Rank and reproduction in cooperatively breeding African wild dogs: behavioral and endocrine correlates. *Behavioral Ecology,* 8, 198–306.

Geffen, E., Gompper, M.E., Gittleman, J.L., Kuh, K-W., MacDonald, D.W. and Wayne, R.K. (1996) Size, life-history traits, and social organization in the Canidae: a re-evaluation. *The American Naturalist,* 147, 140–60.

Girman, D.J., Mills, M.G.L., Geffen, E. and Wayne, R.K. (1997) A molecular genetic analysis of social structure, dispersal, and interpack relationships of the African wild dog (*Lycaon pictus*). *Behavioral Ecology and Sociobiology,* 40, 187–98.

Haase, E. (2000) Comparison of reproductive biological parameters in male wolves and domestic dogs. Zeitschrift für Säugetierkunde. *International Journal of Mammalian Biology,* 65, 257–70.

Robbins, R.L. and McCreery, K.E. (2000) Dominant female cannibalism in the African wild dog. *African Journal of Ecology,* 38, 91–2.

Sillero-Zubiri, C., Johnson, P.J. and MacDonald, D.W. (1998) A hypothesis for breeding synchrony in Ethiopian wolves (*Canis simensis*). *Journal of Mammology*, 79, 853–8.

Smith, D., Meier, T., Geffen, E., Mech, L.D., Burch, J.W., Adams, L.G. and Wayne, R.K. (1997) Is incest common in gray wolf packs? *Behavioral Ecology*, 8, 384–91.

Tannerfeldt, M. and Angerbjorn, A. (1998) Fluctuating resources and the evolution of litter size in the arctic fox. *Oikos*, 83, 545–59.

Venkataraman, A.B. (1998) Male-biased adult sex ratios and their significance for cooperative breeding in dhole, *Cuon alpinus*, packs. *Ethology*, 104, 671–84.

Chapter 7   Hunting

Bueler, L.E. (1973) *Wild Dogs of the World*. Stein and Day Publishers, New York.

Corbett, L. (1995) *The Dingo in Australia and Asia*. University of New South Wales Press, Sydney.

Creel, S. and Creel, N.M. (1995) Communal hunting and pack size in African wild dogs, *Lycaon pictus*. *Animal Behaviour*, 50, 1325–39.

Fanshawe, J.H. and Fitzgibbon, C.D. (1993) Factors influencing the hunting success of an African wild dog pack. *Animal Behaviour*, 45, 479–90.

Fox, M. W. (1984) *The Whistling Hunters. Field Studies of the Asiatic Wild Dog (Cuon Alpinus)*. State University of New York Press, Albany, NY.

Gittleman, J.L. (ed.) (1989) *Carnivore Behavior, Ecology, and Evolution*. Cornell University Press (Comstock Publishing Associates), New York.

Johnsingh, A.J.T. (1982) Reproductive and social behaviour of the dhole, (*Cuon alpinus* Canidae). *Journal of Zoology, London*, 198, 443–63.

Kleiman, D.G. and Eisenberg, J.F. (1973) Comparison of canid and felid social systems from an evolutionary perspective. *Animal Behaviour*, 21, 637–59.

Spirit of the Wild Dog

MacDonald, D.W. and Courtenay, O. (1996) Enduring social relationships in a population of crab-eating zorros, *Cerdocyon thous*, in Amazonian Brazil (Carnivora, Canidae). *Journal of Zoology, London*, 239, 329–55.

Packer, C. and Caro, T.M. (1997) Foraging costs in social carnivores. *Animal Behaviour*, 54, 1317–18.

Vincent, L.E. and Bekoff, M. (1978) Quantitative analyses of the ontogeny of predatory behaviour in coyotes, *Canis latrans*. *Animal Behaviour*, 26, 225–31.

Wrangham, R. and Peterson, D. (1996) *Demonic Males. Apes and the Origins of Human Violence*. Bloomsbury Publishing, London.

Chapter 8   Intelligent behaviour

Agnetta, B., Hare, B. and Tomasello, M. (2000) Cues to food location that domestic dogs (*Canis familiaris*) of different ages do and do not use. *Animal Cognition*, 3, 107–12.

Avital, E. and Jablonka, E. (1994) Social learning and the evolution of behaviour. *Animal Behaviour*, 48, 1195–9.

Boesch, C. and Boesch, H. (1990) Tool use and tool making in wild chimpanzees. *Folia Primatologica*, 54, 86–9.

Box, H. and Gibson, K. (eds) (1999) *Mammalian Social learning: Comparative and Ecological Perspectives*. Cambridge University Press, Cambridge.

Braastad, B.O. (1998) Effects of prenatal stress on behaviour of offspring of laboratory and farmed mammals. *Applied Animal Behaviour Science*, 61, 159–80.

Coppinger, R. and Coppinger, L. (2001) *Dogs: A Startling New Understanding of Canine Origin, Behavior, and Evolution*. Scribner, New York.

Coren, S. (1994) *The Intelligence of Dogs: Canine Consciousness and Capabilities*. The Free Press, New York.

Fiset, S., Gagnon, S. and Beaulieu, C. (2000) Spatial coding of hidden objects in dogs (*Canis familiaris*). *Journal of Comparative Psychology*, 114, 315–24.

Selected reading

Fox, M. W. (1971) *Behaviour of Wolves, Dogs and Related Canids.* Jonathan Cape, London.

Hall, R.L. and Sharp, H.S. (1978) *Wolf and Man: Evolution in Parallel.* Academic Press, New York.

Hare, B.H. and Tomasello, M. (1999) Domestic dogs (*Canis familiaris*) use human and conspecific social cues to locate hidden food. *Journal of Comparative Psychology*, 113, 173–7.

Hare, B.H., Call, J. and Tomasello, M. (1998) Communication of food location between human and dog (*Canis familiaris*). *Evolution of Communication*, 2, 137–59.

Hunt, G.R. (2000) Human-like, population-level specialization in the manufacture of pandanus tools by New Caledonian crows, *Corvus moneduloides. Proceedings of the Royal Society, London B*, 267, 403–13.

McKinley, J. and Sambrook, T.D. (2000) Use of human cues given by domestic dogs (*Canis familiaris*) and horses (*Equus caballus*). *Animal Cognition*, 3, 13–22.

Miklósi, A., Polgárdi, R., Topál, J. and Csányi, V. (1998) Use of experimenter-given cues in dogs. *Animal Cognition*, 1, 113–21.

Miklósi, A., Polgárdi, R., Topál, J. and Csányi, V. (2000) Intentional behavior in dog-human communication: An experimental analysis of 'showing' behavior in the dog. *Animal Cognition*, 3, 159–66.

Pongrácz, P., Miklósi, A., Kubinyi, E., Gurobi, K., Topál, J. and Csányi, V. (2001) Social learning in dogs: the effect of human demonstrator on the performance of dogs in a detour task. *Animal Behaviour*, 62, 1109–17.

Povinelli, D.J. and Eddy, T.J. (1996) Factors influencing young chimpanzees' recognition of 'attention'. *Journal of Comparative Psychology*, 110, 336–45.

Rogers, L.J. (1997) *Minds of Their Own: Thinking and Awareness in Animals.* Allen & Unwin, Sydney.

Rogers, L.J. and Kaplan, G. (1998) *Not Only Roars and Rituals.* Allen & Unwin, Sydney.

Soprini, K., Miklósi, A., Topál, J. and Csányi, V. (2001) Comprehension of human communicative signs in pet dogs (*Canis familiaris*). *Journal of Comparative Psychology*, 115, 122–6.

Chapter 9 Domestic and feral dogs

Boitani, L. (1983) Wolf and dog competition in Italy. *Acta Zoologica Fennica*, 174, 259–64.

Boitani, L. and Ciucci, P. (1995) Comparative social ecology of feral dogs and wolves. *Ethology, Ecology and Evolution*, 7, 49–72.

Clutton-Brock, J. (1981) *Domesticated Animals for Early Times*. Heinemann, London.

Clutton-Brock, J. (1999) *A Natural History of Domesticated Mammals*, 2nd edn. Cambridge University Press, Cambridge.

Coppinger, R. and Coppinger, L. (2001) *Dogs: A Startling New Understanding of Canine Origin, Behavior, and Evolution*. Scribner, New York.

Corbett, L.K. (1985) Morphological comparisons of Australian and Thai dingoes: a reappraisal of dingo status, distribution and ancestry. *Proceedings of the Ecological Society of Australia*, 13, 277–91.

Corbett, L.K. (2001) *The Dingo in Australia and Asia*. J.B. Books, South Australia.

Fleming, P., Corbett, L. Harden, R. and Thomson, P. (2001) *Managing the Impacts of Dingoes and Other Wild Dogs*. Bureau of Rural Sciences, Canberra.

Fox, M. W. (1978) *The Dog: Its Domestication and Behavior*. Garland STPM Press, New York.

Gottelli, D., Sillero-Zubiri, C., Applebaum, G.D., Roy, M.S., Girman, D.J., Garciá-Moreno, J., Ostrander, E.A. and Wayne, R.K. (1994) Molecular genetics of the most endangered canid: the Ethiopian wolf, *Canis simenis*. *Molecular Ecology*, 3, 301–12.

Newby, J. (1997) *The Pact for Survival*. ABC Books, Sydney.

Newsome, A.E. and Corbett, L.K. (1982) The identity of the dingo. II. Hybridisation with domestic dogs in captivity and in the wild. *Australian Journal of Zoology*, 30, 365–74.

Newsome, A.E., Corbett, L.K. and Carpenter, S.M. (1980) The identity of the dingo. I. Morphological discriminants of dingo and dogs skulls. *Australian Journal of Zoology*, 28, 615–25.

Paxton, D.W. (2000) A case for a naturalistic perspective. *Anthrozoös*, 13, 5–8.

Selected reading

Randi, E., Lucchini, V., Christensen, M.F., Mucci, N., Funk, S.M., Dolf, G. and Loeschcke, V. (2000) Mitochondrial DNA variability in Italian and East European wolves: detecting the consequences of small population size and hybridisation. *Conservation Biology*, 14, 464–73.

Reardon, M. (1993) Dingo: creature of the senses, master of the night. *Australian Geographic*, 32, 84–9.

Ruvinsky, A. and Sampson, J. (2001) *The Generics of the Dog.* CABI Publishing, Wallingford.

Schwartz, M. (1997) *A History of Dogs in the Early Americas.* Yale University Press, New Haven.

Serpell, J. (1995) *The Domestic Dog: Its Evolution, Behaviour and Interactions with People.* Cambridge University Press, Cambridge.

Shigehara, N., Guoqin, Q., Komiya, H. and Jing, Y. (1998) Morphological study of the ancient dogs from three Neolithic sites in China. *International Journal of Osteoarchaeology*, 8, 11–22.

Taçon, P.S.C. and Pardoe, C. (2002) Dogs make us human. *Nature Australia*, 27 (4), 53–61.

Vila, C. and Wayne, R.K. (1999) Hybridization between wolves and dogs. *Conservation Biology*, 13, 195–8.

Vila, C., Savolainen, P., Maldonado, J.E., Amorin, I.R., Rice, J.E., Honeycutt, R.L., Crandall, K.A., Lundeberg, J. and Wayne, R.K. (1997) Multiple ancient origins of the domestic dog. *Science*, 276, 1687–9.

Wilton, A.N., Steward, D.J. and Zafiris, K. (1999) Microsatellite variation in the Australian dingo. *Journal of Heredity*, 90, 108–11.

Chapter 10   Future of the wild dog

Allen, L. (2000) Dingo enigma. *Wildlife Australia Magazine*, autumn, 16–19.

Andelt, W. F., Phillips, R.L. Gruver, K.S. and Guthrie, J.W. (1999) Coyote predation on domestic sheep deterred with electronic dog-training collar. *Wildlife Society Bulletin*, 27, 12–17.

Anderson, R.M. (1986) Vaccination of wildlife reservoirs. *Nature*, 322, 304–5.

Arthur, L.M. (1981) Coyote control: the public response. *Journal of Range Management*, 34, 14–15.

Baker, P. J., Funk, S.M. Stephen, H. and White, P.C.L. (2000) Flexible spatial organization of urban foxes, *Vulpes vulpes*, before and during an outbreak of sarcoptic mange. *Animal Behaviour*, 59, 127–46.

Corbett, L. (1995) Dingoes: expatriate wolves or native dogs? *Nature Australia*, 25, 46–55.

Courchamp, F., Rasmussen, G.S.A. and Macdonald, D.W. (2002) Small pack size imposes a trade-off between hunting and pup-guarding in the painted hunting dog, *Lycaon pictus*. *Behavioral Ecology*, 13, 20–7.

Creel, S. and Creel, N.M. (1996) Limitation of African wild dogs by competition with larger carnivores. *Conservation Biology*, 10, 526–38.

Fleming, P., Corbett, L. Harden, R. and Thomson, P. (2001) *Managing the Impacts of Dingoes and Other Wild Dogs*. Bureau of Rural Sciences, Canberra.

Forbes, G.J. and Theberge, J.B. (1996) Cross-boundary management of Algonquin Park wolves. *Conservation Biology*, 10, 1091–7.

Haber, G.C. (1996) Biological, conservation, and ethical implications of exploiting and controlling wolves. *Conservation Biology*, 10, 1068–81.

Karanth, K.U. and Sunquist, M.E. (2000) Behavioural correlates of predation by tiger (*Panthera tigris*), leopard (*Panthera pardus*) and dhole (*Cuon alpinus*) in Nagarahole, India. *Journal of Zoology, London*, 250, 255–65.

Knight, J. (2001) If they could talk to the animals. *Nature*, 414, 246–7.

Knowlton, F.F., Gese, E.M. and Jaeger, M.M. (1999) Coyote depredation control: an interface between biology and management. *Journal of Range Management*, 52, 398–409.

Mills, M.G.L. and Gorman, M.L. (1997) Factors affecting the density and distribution of wild dogs in the Krüger National Park. *Conservation Biology* 11, 1397–406.

Selected reading

Phillips, M. (1995) Conserving the red wolf. *Canid News* 3,
    http://www.canids.org/PUBLICAT/CNNEWS/consredw.htm
ProPaw (2001) Poison Facts.
    http://www.volunteerinfo.org/propaw/poison.htm.
Reynolds, J.C. and Tapper, S. C. (1996) Control of mammalian
    predators in game management and conservation. *Mammal
    Revues*, 26, 127–56.
Saunders, G., Coman, B.J. Kinnear, J. and Braysher, M. (1995)
    Managing Vertebrate Pests: Foxes. Government Publishing
    Service, Canberra.
Vila, C. and Wayne, R.K. (1999) Hybridization between wolves and
    dogs. *Conservation Biology*, 13, 195–8.
Vucetich, J.A. and Creel, S. (1999) Ecological interactions, social
    organization, and extinction risk in African wild dogs.
    Conservation Biology, 13, 1172–82.
Woodroffe, R. and Ginsberg, J.R. (1999) Conserving the African wild
    dog *Lycaon pictus*. I. Diagnosing and treating causes of decline.
    Oryx , 33, 132–42.
Woodroffe, R. and Ginsberg. J.R. (1999) Conserving the African wild
    dog, *Lycaon pictus*. II. Is there a role for reintroduction? *Oryx*,
    33, 143–51.

Index

Page numbers in *italics* refer to photographs or maps

Index

Index

Index

Index

Index